Printed in the United Kingdom

First Printing, 2020

ISBN 978-1-5272-5859-4

Marriage

&

Ego Within

Bazi Bussuri

Marital Illiteracy Publications

Contents

Acknowledgements

I remember as a child, the elders saying to us "He who does not thank people, does not thank Allah". This was their way of showing us the importance of expressing gratitude to those who helped us. As social beings, our very human survival depends on helping one another. We reach our goals only with the help of others.

I give my thanks and express my heartfelt gratitude to all those who have helped me starting with my parents, my wife and children and my teachers of all levels "who put up with me" and supported me all the way. Also, special thanks to my work colleagues and friends for helping me with the proof reading and mental support.

A very special thanks to Mina Daum who voluntarily offered me to proofread and edit my work. She made a valuable contribution to my work and I am indebted to her. Also, to my best friend Ahmed Amin who was always reminding me to finish this book and stop procrastinating. He also helped me with the design of this beautiful book cover.

Finally, a very special thanks to local libraries in Newham, Redbridge and Tower Hamlets for providing valuable books. Part of the ingredients of this book is the notes taken from their books. Additionally, many thanks to all authors of the books and articles I read. All these contributors mentioned will be rewarded by Allah Inshaa Allah. May Allah make this book beneficial to all.

Introduction

You need companions in all different areas of your life, but there is nothing like the companionship of a marriage.

The greatest asset of a nation is its people. Economists call this 'human capital', and it is the quality, not the quantity, of the people that is most important. Typically, people are nurtured at home, school and the religious institutions, and the qualities people possess are dependent on what happens in these three places. For instance, if we get our first and most important environment (home/marriage) wrong, we will struggle to improve the quality of our life, and this negatively impacts our development.

Therefore, it is vital to educate our children for life, including their emotional relationship with themselves and others, and not for work only. For example, it is important to educate people about the marital relationship, as marriage is a promise, not just between the couple but to the community at large, to generations past and to those yet to be born.

I got married at the age of eighteen knowing little to nothing about marital relationships. Three months before the ceremony, as most people do, I began to ask advice from people who were already married, such as the customers of my father's wholesale business, neighbours and relatives. But most of their advice was focused on performing better in bed during the honeymoon, and especially the first night. Some would tell me, 'a month before the ceremony, make sure you eat camel's meat fried with sesame oil'. Another person told me, have pure honey with two raw eggs every morning', as if I was preparing for a boxing match.

Their argument was that if you perform well in bed during the honeymoon, your marriage will be successful. Mastering the physical, rather than the emotional aspects was seen as the key factor. After I had been married for two years, the civil war in Somalia broke out. We fled to Kenya and from there to United Kingdom.

Normally the first two years of the marriage is a honeymoon period, and everything is idealised. The reality of our relationship began once we arrived in the UK, a different country, culture and environment that demanded a great deal of perseverance and tolerance on our parts. This was the period where the spouses begin to assert themselves; some might call it a period of adjustment. I acknowledged the need for a change of attitude and the relationship meant a lot to me. I also knew that the change had to come from me before I tried to change my wife. Change is possible and easier when you gain self-awareness.

It is well said that *"the greatest gift you can give to somebody is your personal development"*. But I had no valuable knowledge about what changes were necessary; the problem is that many of us are not good at this and nobody taught us how to do it. We never had a class at school on how to resolve conflict in relationships.

Our schooling system was based on the needs of industrialisation and the skills we gain from school were mostly on how to accomplish and acquire, but not how to *be*. We all know how to maintain our physical health and how to practice dental hygiene by 'brushing twice a day'. We have known it since we were five years old. But we do not know about maintaining our psychological health (emotional hygiene). We spend more time taking care of our teeth than we do our minds. We sustain psychological injuries even more often than we do physical ones; injuries such as like failure, rejection or loneliness.

These difficulties can also get worse if we ignore them, and they can dramatically impact our lives, especially our marriages. We cannot expect children to grow up and get along on an ever more crowded planet if we do not prepare them. It is even vital for them to learn at this modern era that has caused the biggest identity crises in the history of humankind.

Our industrial-based education has created a culture that encourages us to think about how to have a great career but leaves many of us inarticulate about how to cultivate the inner life. Such culture gives little encouragement to exercise humility, sympathy and self-confrontation, all of which are necessary for building character. We need to teach our children the laws of emotion that explain to you, your own inner world and the complex world of interpersonal dynamics. It is easier to learn this emotional intelligence and self-awareness during childhood, similar to learning languages. This will make them so much more comfortable in their own skin in marital life.

But with a "Big ME" attitude, a marital relationship will crumple, as this attitude goes against the moral logic of the following:

- In order to fulfil yourself, you need to forget your ego-self.
- You have to give to receive.
- In order to find yourself, you have to lose yourself.

The turning point for me was when I travelled to Saudi Arabia for *Hajj* in 2004. After completing my hajj duties, our group had an extra ten days to stay in Makkah before we arrived back in London. This was possibly because, that was the cheaper option for the tour operator, as the tickets are cheaper at that time. So, everyone in the group had 10 idle days to stay in the hotel, go to Haram to pray, walk around the city and come back to eat. I saw a book shop inside the shopping mall opposite the Masjid. I went in, looking for a book to read during the 10 days.

I browsed through the shelves and bought a book in Arabic by an author called Istambuli, entitled *Brides Boon*, and started reading. Whilst reading the book, I felt like someone who has found his first diamond, I couldn't put it down. I realised how illiterate I was in my marital relationship. Acknowledging my lack of marital understanding was my biggest hurdle and this made me thirstier to read and enquire.

The understanding that I had on the overall marital relationship was very shallow and shaped by the philosophy of the world and local tradition rather than by the principles of the Quran and the Sunnah of Prophet Muhammad SAW. Such lack of marital literacy leads most of our marriages to be empty of tranquillity (*Mawadah*) that was guaranteed by Allah in the Quran. Our society's failure to train people to meet the needs of the other, especially the needs of one's marriage partner, has played a large part in our high divorce rate.

I do not have many regrets in life, but the one thing I really regretted was not making reading a habit at a younger age. It is different and more effective than watching a programme on screen. For example, reading literature about the life of Prophet Muhammad SAW and his companions is in fact the greatest time saver, as it gives us access to a range of emotions and events that would take years, decades and even millennia to try to experience directly.

Reading is the greatest reality simulator as it puts you infinitely more situations than you can ever witness or experience directly. I would recommend that you make reading a habit in your daily life and do it consistently. After arriving to London, I began to act upon what I had read, chapter by chapter, in my own life. It was not easy, but to my surprise, my wife said to me "I think Hajj changed you", meaning that it had made me a better husband. It is true Hajj as well as the book helped me change my undesirable behaviours as a husband.

I also had a burning desire to change, and Allah helped me with my good intention. It is always good to make steps towards change, however small; it will pay off in the end. The breakthrough will not happen instantly, but gradually. Taking smaller steps to achieve the bigger task of inner personal growth remains the best approach.

It did not stop there; I had a few copies of the same book in English and started to give them to young local brothers who were planning to marry. They were grateful to read and thanked me for helping them lay good foundations for their marriages. So, every now and then, when I go to Umrah, I always buy five copies of the book and give it to the local youth who are thinking about getting married. Finally, someone told me that there was a free PDF version of the book online, after which I told them to read it online. To me however, reading from a book is more effective and easier to digest than reading it on a screen.

My actions led the local youth to refer me as the 'marriage man', since every time they see me, the word 'marriage' pops into their mind. Marriage to me is not a simple social institution that everyone enters into because they fall in love and live happily ever after. It is the oldest institution starting from Adam and Eve and it is not something to throw yourself haphazardly.

At a very young age, children should be trained to meet the needs and expectations that they will encounter if and when they enter marriage. Studies have shown that children are much more likely to copy their parents' actions than their words. Parents are the best educators for children when it comes to marital relationships. We inherit many of our habits, reactions and inner voices from our parents. But the truth is they might not have been a good model of conflict resolution, because nobody taught them. This is leading us to use failed recipes in our own lives.

Many of us may view ourselves as different from our mother and father. However, the more closely we observe and examine our attitudes and behaviours, the more we see how many of their psychological issues and solutions have been passed on to us. Our parents too carried many of the reactions of their parents and so on, passed on from generation to generation.

We become entangled in a story about us that we never meant to write. Without knowing it, we absorb ways of being a wife or husband from our family of origin—and we form standards for our spouse to live up to in his or her role, too. That's why marriages collapse. However, we are now too old to blame our parents for any of our marital shortcomings. We need to move on and work on ourselves and release some of the inherited traditional habits that negatively impact our marriages.

This is a noble act that prevents destructive patterns of behaviour from being passed on to the next generation. For instance, many of our children have not yet witnessed us practising the Prophetic Sunnah, the Blessed Prophet said: "Even to put a morsel of food into your wife's mouth is a Sadaqah". For children to see their father putting food into their mother's mouth is the best gift they could ever get. Children flourish when the quality of your marital relation is good.

There is a saying, "inside every child is an emotional tank waiting to be filled with love". When a child really feels loved, he or she will develop normally, but when the love tank is empty, the child will misbehave. Much of the misbehaviour of children is motivated by the craving of an empty "Love tank". The most important thing a father can do for his children is to love their mother, as this will have more long-lasting effect than buying them the latest gadgets. The same is true for the mother.

Few of us have ever tried this Sunnah, but child psychology experts acknowledge that such assurance gives the child an emotional intelligence and the feeling of optimism in their daily life. The emotional need for love does not end in childhood. It follows us into adulthood and into marriage. It is fundamental to our nature, and the need to be loved and respected by one's spouse is at the heart of marital desires.

Many of the brothers complain about the consistent nagging of their wives, but what the sisters are indirectly saying by nagging is "give me some reassurance that you love me". However, many of us fail to reassure or express the love we have for our wives, even though we love them so much. We need to express this love regardless of current circumstances. Love should be unconditional, which means dealing with the other person's insecurities, thoughts and fears, even when you don't want to.

This form of love is also far more satisfying, meaningful and brings true happiness, not just another series of 'highs'. Your love should not be conditional upon your partner helping you feel better about yourself. Such conditionality prevents any true, deep-level intimacy from emerging. You need to love with imagination, i.e. to imagine the positive reasons why others are behaving as they are. It is well said, "Love unconditionally, but rely only on yourself."

In loving relationships, it is normal for both people to occasionally sacrifice their own desires, needs, and time for one another. But it is not okay to sacrifice one's self-respect and one's dignity. A loving relationship is supposed to supplement our individual identity, not damage it or replace it. I recall one traditional elder who once advised me not to inform my wife about my love for her, as it would make her more controlling.

But in reality, our wives get irritated and frustrated when we fail to reassure them of our love for them. Showing our wives, the love we have for them drives them to be the best of themselves and leads them stand by us in any circumstances. Expressing your love for your partner in words, giving gifts, helping each another, and having quality time and physical touch were the Sunnah of our Prophet Muhammed SAW. We are wired for connections and marriage fuelled with love and respect provide us with a greater sense of meaning and happiness than any other human experience.

Similarly, sisters complain about how their husbands are withdrawn. What the brothers are expressing through this withdrawal is, "Give me the respect that enables me to express my love to you". Love and respect are vital for both partners, like oxygen to a suffocating person. But women give more value to love, while a man's deepest desire is to be respected.

Research has shown that many men would rather live with a wife who respects but does not love them than live with a wife who loves them but does not respect them. When a husband is shown respect, he feels motivated to show his wife the kind of unconditional love she desires. To respect a man means to admire him, and a man interprets respect as love. When a woman tells him, she loves him it doesn't mean anything to him. But when she respects him, he knows she loves him.

To respect means to speak highly of, to hold in high regard and to praise. But the problem is that our homes contain no praise, and that is not good. Even if the person is not praiseworthy, we still need to praise. From this respect comes everything else – trust, patience, perseverance. Respect is vital for both wife and husband. There are times when you won't feel love for your partner. But you never want to lose respect for your partner. Once you lose respect you will never get it back.

True respect for one another is the only thing that can save and cushion both from marital collapse. Without that bedrock of respect beneath you, you will doubt each other's intentions. You will judge your partner's choices and encroach on their independence. You will feel the need to hide things from one another for fear of criticism. And this is when the cracks of marital collapse begin to show. For your marriage to thrive, each partner needs an inner state of mind full of humility. Humility is not thinking less of yourself; humility is thinking about yourself less.

Beyond this, the aim of this book is to give you a foundation to strengthen and improve the quality of your marriage and act as a genuine soulmate. To achieve this goal, one must acknowledge that there is a price to pay in having a marital relationship. People say, "a precious stone cannot be polished without friction, nor can man be perfected without trials." Social reform always starts with the individual; as the Quran says, "Indeed, Allah will not change the condition of a people until they change what is in themselves".

Changing yourself here means changing your bad behaviour and habits into good ones. There is no self to change, you will be always you and you are your identity. Always remember, you and your spouse are like a sandwich; in marital life, you are one slice, he or she is the other. What you put in between the slices is up to you. The purpose of this book is to help you make the sandwich of your marital life tastier and avoid making it sour. The promise of marital tranquillity is clearly stated in the Quran, but it is subject to your approach as couples.

This book is divided into three main chapters, each with small subsections. The first chapter highlights how to handle conflicts constructively. Chapter Two sets out the benefits of well-managed marital conflict. Chapter three offers prescriptions for good character traits which, if put in practice, can immunise your marriage from negativity and lead to tranquillity. At the end, what many people are accomplish is due to the relationships that they have. That was the most important marker for their health, well-being and meaning in their lives.

Today, as society transforms, marital relationships are also constantly changing at a rapid pace and it is making many anxious. We must confront the source of the anxiety and identify an appropriate course of action. We have to face the uncertainty and massive self-doubt that was created by the collapse of our social system and the introduction of romantic consumerism and emotional capitalism.

The most important thing to be aware of is that we as humans are broken, insecure and scared and yet designed for joy. Only by coming to terms with our brokenness, can we build from the pieces a house of joy. Always be grateful for what you have and try not to compare your insides to their outsides. Because this makes you much worse than you already are. Even if you get to know those you are comparing with, they turn out to have plenty of irritability and shadow of their own. The lesson here is that it is necessary to forgive yourselves and others constantly.

Chapter 2

How to constructively approach
Marital Conflict

"Marital Conflict is a must; it is like
rain. Put up with it to witness Marital
Rainbow "*Mawadah*"

Conflict in Marriage is Inevitable

When you are young you assume life is a straight line; you go to school, then university, you start your career, you get married, and everything goes smoothly. So, when you are faced with adversity such as marital conflict, it comes as a shock. Initially couples find each other irresistible, and only start to feel as if they are incompatible if they fail to meet each other's basic needs.

What happens is that, as the euphoria of honeymoon evaporates little by little and runs its course, we return to the world of reality and we begin to assert ourselves. It is important to inform our young people that adversity is a fact of life. It can't be controlled. What we can control is how we react to it. It has been said that the darkest hour of the night comes just before the dawn, and after that sunlight starts to emerge. Unfortunately, many of us give up on our marriages during the last hour before the dawn.

Had we waited a little and faced the conflict in a constructive manner, we would have witnessed the dawn of beauty that always comes after night. There are no negatives in life; only challenges to overcome that will make you stronger. The main obstacle is fear of feeling vulnerable or being exposed, and this stops us from taking such constructive steps. We then end up becoming defensive, distant and demanding.

But it is a fact that many people end up growing and developing into stronger people due to their past pains. It's not the survival of trauma or difficult times that makes you stronger, it's the work you put in as a result of the trauma that makes you stronger. Research shows that 90% of people who experience a traumatic event also experience at least one form of personal growth in the following months and years.

It is worthwhile to face short-term pain for greater gain in the future. Two things we should never do in marital conflict are to Avoid or to Appease. By 'avoid' I refer to those who say, "I just want to sweep everything under the carpet and never rock the marriage boat". 'Appeasing' refers to those who say, "I always give in, peace at any price". The worst thing in life is to get married and live at an emotional distance from the person you are married to for the rest of your life. Isolation is devastating to the human psyche.

Within three days of social isolation, the mind descends into confusion, anger and ultimately apathy. Marital conflict is like monsoon water accumulating on a flat roof. You don't realise it's up there, but it gets heavier until one day, with a great crash, the roof collapses. The best way is to face the strong wind of marital conflict the same manner the aeroplane faces the wind to fly. We should not run away from marital wind and rather use it to take us to the greater beyond of marital tranquillity.

When you look back on those experiences of the ups and downs in your marital life, your main conclusion will mostly be that it was worthwhile experience. Looking back on those events affords you the luxury to reflect both about the experience and yourself.

Next page is a summary of the six steps you need to deal with marital conflict constructively.

Step 1 "Make the first move and ask Allah for Guidance"

Taking the first initiative is the most important point of resolving conflict and it pleases Allah. Be a peace maker and not a peacekeeper, and do not wait for the other person. Conflict is never resolved accidently; it just does not happen and is always a result of deliberate action.

Reconciliation must be the priority; do it at once, no matter whether you are the offender or the offended against. According to Islamic teachings it is not permissible for a man to forsake his brother for more than three days, each of them turning away from the other when they meet "**in cases where the forsaking is caused by anger with regard to something permissible**". For couples it is even more important. Such turning away blocks as well as affects the acceptance of your prayers, worship and your own happiness. It is not a good habit to sleep with a feeling of grievances at night.

Delaying before resolving conflict has further negative consequences. Marital conflict is an emotional wound that needs to be treated straight away. If it is not treated straight away, both of you bleed emotionally, leading to emotional infection. Your mind will absorb all the negative thoughts and this creates an unrealistically negative picture of your spouse.

The problem is that the longer it goes on, the more real and believable your negative assumptions will become. These layers of negative assumptions that were formed when you stopped talking to each other will make resolving the conflict harder and harder. 'In marital battles, you do not need to win, you need to end the battle.' Therefore, we must deal with conflict immediately. When you run away from all your problems, you eventually run from yourself. You forget the person you could be if you stayed in one place, worked through your downfalls, accepted your shortcomings and then overcame them.

Step 2 "Feel with your Partner"

During marital problems, we may say to our spouse "I feel for you", but that is not enough. We need to say, "I feel *with* you". When you feel *with* someone, you genuinely empathize with the person, and that leads to an action to resolve the conflict. Effective listening is the best tool to demonstrate empathy towards your partner.

This means paying close attention and focusing on the feelings, not the facts. This will convey the message that you care about and value his/her opinion, and that the relationship matters to you. No matter how angry you have grown with each other, when one yells, the other one should listen. Because when two people yell, there is no communication, just noise and bad vibrations. Always begin with sympathy, not solutions; this is a common mistake that men make.

The capacity to put yourself in your partner's shoes and see the world from his or her perspective enables your marriage to flourish. Therefore, it is better not to ask how the wounded one feels; instead, you yourself, *become* the wounded one. Showing empathy leads you to touch your spouse not just with your hands but with your heart. Respecting other people's feelings, including your partner's, does wonders. It might mean nothing to you, but it could mean everything to them.

It helps him/her to acknowledge his/her own worth. After all, no one can perceive a sense of his own worth until it has been reflected back onto him in the mirror of another loving, caring human being. It is not an easy thing to do, to feel *with* someone, and it takes courage to suppress your ego and accept your vulnerability. But Vulnerability is the birthplace of love, belonging, joy, courage, empathy, and creativity. It is the source of hope, empathy and accountability.

Step 3 "Acknowledge your part of the Conflict"

"We easily see what is done to us before we see what we are doing to our partner"

Relationship math suggests that it is rare for two people to enter marriage and for one person to be responsible for everything that goes wrong. Admitting your own mistakes is the best way to begin in resolving the conflict and demonstrates that you are serious about the relationship.

This represents huge emotional healing and gives the relationship a fresh start. When you start off acknowledging your part in the conflict, your partner will pay more attention to your words and trust will emerge; and this will prevent him/her from causing you harm or loss. Words like "I'm sorry for any pain or hurt I have caused you" can create a breakthrough in resolving conflicts. We should regret our mistakes and learn from them.

We should not let our own tears blind you to the tears of your partner. Admitting our mistakes quickly and with enthusiasm is a lot better than defending yourself. By fighting you never get enough, but by yielding you get more than expected. Whenever you are about to find fault with someone, ask yourself the following question:

What fault of mine most nearly resembles the one I am about to blame? There will always be a part we have played in escalating the conflict. Looking at our own contribution to the conflict is hard. Especially when we genuinely believe it's the other person's responsibility that things got difficult or the problem occurred. One of the reasons it's hard is because we usually look at the situation only through our own version of the story. But by considering our own contribution to the conflict, as well as the other person's, we free ourselves up to more fully understand the situation. This usually leads to satisfying resolution to the conflict.

Step 4 "Focus on the problem, not the Person"

This involves being hard on the problem and soft on the person. Failing to do that leads you to become hostage to your emotions, and you will be consumed with apportioning the blame. There is a world of difference between complaint and criticism. A complaint only addresses a specific action at which your spouse failed. A criticism is more global and consists of negative words about your spouse's character or personality.

The danger with finger-pointing is that it changes the issue into an escalating need to be right. Both spouses fall into a trap that being right is more important than the relationship. Avoid using toxic phrases like *"You always..."* or *"You never..."*. Choose your words wisely; it is well said, "Raise your words, not your voice. It is rain that grows flowers, not thunder." The goal is to come to a satisfactory agreement, not to prove yourself right.

If done correctly, arguing can be a pathway to growth and problem solving. For example, it is better to talk about your feelings when you are not in an angry frame of mind, i.e. when you or your partner can approach the situation with clarity, and deal with it in a constructive manner. Sometimes things just need to be verbalised, and most arguments can be avoided if your partner understands how you feel. Always avoid stockpiling other past issues.

This is where you bring up issues from the past to use as a hammer against whatever problem your partner has asked for help with. Deal with their issue first, and if you really have unresolved feelings from past problems, talk about them another time. If the issue is taken personally, addressing the issue can become emotional and the process can get out of control. The relationship will then become a land mine of unfinished wounds that bleed again at the slightest scratch.

Step 5 "Cooperate as much as possible"

Husbands and wives were meant to be happy as they face life's challenges together, and cooperation not competition is the way forward. This involves working for a common purpose to maintain an extraordinary relationship through the challenges of everyday life. Many of us think we are good at cooperation, but in reality we may be terrible at it. Cooperation requires practice and thankfully, it's a skill that can be learned.

To practice cooperation, married couples are encouraged to engage in "couple projects." This might include making a meal together, painting a room, gardening, or assembling furniture together. The key to cooking or painting or doing other things together is communicating. Food for instance, brings people together and allows you to be on the same page. "To be on the same page, we need to be in the same book."

You were placed on this earth to create, not to compete. The only thing that will redeem mankind is cooperation. It is through cooperation, rather than conflict, that your greatest successes will be derived. Cooperation in marital life is a matter of survival. The real-world faces and will continue to face significant problems and crises that can only be solved through cooperation.

Without taking opportunities to cooperate, we run the risk of ruining our marriages. Anyone who imagines they can work alone winds up surrounded by nothing but rivals, without companions. Cooperation allows us to solve problems that are too complex for anyone to solve individually. We need the assistance of others to be born into this world and to leave it. Any success between those two points is similarly a result of cooperation. A strong marriage requires two people who choose to love each other and work together to better their marriage.

Step 6 "Emphasise Reconciliation not Resolution"

Reconciliation focuses on the relationship, while resolution focuses on the problem. When focusing on reconciliation, the problem loses significance and often becomes irrelevant. We often have legitimate, honest disagreements and differing opinions, but we can disagree without being disagreeable. Allah expects unity, not uniformity; we can walk arm in arm without seeing eye to eye on every issue, and the wisdom is learning how to achieve this. It's always more rewarding to resolve a conflict than to dissolve a relationship.

By simply reminding yourself of your spouse's positive qualities the version of him/her that is good and reliable, even as you grapple with each other's flaws, you can prevent a happy marriage from deteriorating. It is a good practice to start with praise and honest appreciation before you start your reconciliation point with the flaws of your partner. It is always easier to listen un-pleasant things after we have heard some praise of our good points.

Beginning with praise is described as the dentist who begins his/her work with local anaesthetic, to carry on his/her drilling. This allows you tough fruitful conversation and we need tough conversation in our ever-changing social word. Most of things are becoming a matter of negotiation between couples. Marital reconciliation is best achieved when only you and your spouse are involved.

It has to be your idea, not somebody else's. When other people get involved, it will only work when you are willing to reconcile and want the relationship to continue. Always remind yourself the struggle for reconciliation will become a story someday. It will either be a story about why you divorced or a story about how you worked together to build a stronger marriage. You get to decide which story becomes true. Reconciliation is the most powerful yet under-utilised tool we have. It is the only way we can minimise the anger in and anger out moment of both husband and wife. Reconciliation is more beautiful than victory as it takes courage to love through offense.

Chapter 2

Benefits of Constructively approached Marital Conflict

If Allah intends good for someone, then he afflicts him with trials. al-Bukhārī 5321

"Benefit 1 of Marital Conflict "Self-Knowledge"

"Govern yourself and you can govern the world"

Without self-knowledge, a person will not get very far on their spiritual journey, nor will they be able to sustain whatever progress they have made. Marital conflicts, if handled constructively will allow you to understand yourself and such self-knowledge becomes an invaluable guardian against self-deception. No matter how well you think of yourself and your partner beforehand, the first years of marriage are full of surprises, not only about your spouse but about yourself.

Marriage is the embarking point for the greater journey of self-knowledge. It does not put you in a box as some people claim, but it shows us the box we are in. Marital conflict if handled well is something that rocks you back into your inner self. Unfortunately, our view of ourselves is often wrong, as we tend to believe our own press. Transformation happens when our ordinary perspective shifts and we attain new understanding of who we really are.

Our biggest fear is the risk of being truly alive and expressing what we really are. Your own self-realisation is the greatest service you can render the world. Nobody abuses us more than we abuse ourselves, and the way we judge ourselves is the harshest. Moreover, when we are unaware of our own habits, routines, impulses, and reactions, we no longer control them; they control us, and it feels bad within.

That is why psychologists recommend looking within you with a true mirror. When you're looking at a regular mirror you look for reassurance that you're perfect. But when you look in a true mirror, "Looking within", you don't look *at* yourself, you look *for* yourself; you look for revelation, not reassurance.

Marital life with its ups and down makes us realise how important it is for everyone to get real. Let's face it; we all live in our own 'bubble 'or our version of ourselves. Our image of perfection is the reason we reject ourselves and fail to accept the way we are. Also, it is why we do not accept others the way they are. The marital relationship journey can help us to discover who we are and to achieve the best version of ourselves. This process makes us mindful of the types of thoughts that interfere with our ability to tolerate and be patient. You will know that both of you have needs and both needs matter and can easily convey your needs.

For example, if while we are having an argument with our spouse, we suddenly 'catch ourselves in the act' and experience our current state completely and without judgement, something extraordinary can occur. Our awareness of ourselves will expand and the old patterns of the habits of our personality will begin to fall away. We may feel embarrassed when we notice what we are doing. But if we stay present in our discomfort, we will, in the end, get to who we really are (our true essence).

This act of self-analysis will ignite our innate drive to self-realization and will allow us to blossom rather than wither. Such self-awareness leads to self-acceptance, meaning accepting the flaws of your own emotions and thoughts as well as the flaws of others. Alongside this, you will develop the feel of empathy for others, as normally empathy occurs in proportion to your own self-acceptance.

You will be able to look at the flaws in the emotions and minds of others, but rather than judging them or hating them, feel compassion for them. This isn't to say that empathy and compassion will solve all your marital problems. But they certainly will make them better. Because you have come to terms with the flaws in yourself, you will be able to come to terms and forgive those flaws in others.

In fact, you will achieve real love, and this will lead you to learn how to laugh at yourselves and stay lighthearted as our imperfections come to surface. This creates an environment where occasional teasing or kidding around is okay and where you and your spouse feel safe to make observations or suggestions. As both parties begin to feel safe, the relationship has the chance to deepen and grow. Once we understand the nature of our personality's mechanisms and weaknesses, then they stop being weaknesses. We begin to have a choice about identifying with them or not. If we are not aware of them, clearly no choice is possible.

Knowing ourselves makes us fully aware that the quality of life will not improve simply if external factors (i.e. the material world) improve. Therefore, when faced with marital conflict, we should not act on our impulses or let negative feelings dictate our lives. Failing to do that leads us to abuse ourselves and give in to our critical selves, and this feels like serving a life sentence in the dungeon of life.

The Superego is the 'inner critic' that keeps us restricted and alienates us again and again from our true nature. We undermine our own well-being as a result of unconscious disturbances which influence our thoughts and behaviours. For example, someone may experience having very wild, inappropriate negative thoughts that make them wonder why on earth they are thinking like this. It is important to note that this is not real; it is the whispers of Satan, as every one of us has a satanic companion. This is part of being human; we all struggle with insecurities, and these can really hold us back from being engaged in our life.

We are all deeply divided self and the inner struggle against our own weakness is the central drama of life. Therefore, we need to understand and seek refuge from Allah. Seeking refuge from Allah means showing healthy vulnerability and humility in the eyes of Allah; if we can do this, the breakthrough will come. We are complete but enough only with the help of Allah.

During marital conflict, because of the tension and anger, couples can easily fall prey into these negative satanic whispers. If we listen to these satanic whispers, they become beliefs. Therefore, we need to start focusing our attention on the thoughts that run through our mind. Be aware and stay present with those negative thoughts, learn how to let them go and then turn the volume and the noise down on your limiting beliefs. Do not save these negative thoughts in your heart-drive and release them as trees release the wind. Without self-awareness you will become defensive and escalate the argument. It is important to analyse yourself and be your own therapist.

When the Sahaba would experience marital conflict, or even if their horses misbehaved, they used to look back, reflect on and remember if they had committed any sins during the day. Such self-awareness allowed them to understand that sometimes they were responsible for it. This enabled them to excel in life and overcome the *Ego* (the Nafs that urges evil) and move to the stage of *Nafs al-Mutma`inna* (The Nafs at Peace).

Accepting and loving your vulnerable self is a huge task to achieve, but constructively handled marital conflicts lead you there. The poet Khalil Gibran said it beautifully in his quote *"Allah said, "Love Your Enemy," and I obeyed him and loved myself"*. For advice on how to overcome resistance from the enemy within (our inner self) we can turn to Sun Tzu's Art of War for insight. "If you know the enemy and know yourself in 100 battles, there will be no danger; if you know yourself but not the enemy there will be one victory for one loss; but if you know neither the enemy nor yourself, then every battle will lead to certain defeat".

We need to quiet our ego-self and by quieting the self could we see the world clearly. Only by quieting the self could we understand other people and accept what they are offering. We are not strong enough to consistently defeat selfishness, pride, greed and self-deception. Everybody needs redemptive assistance from Allah. This is a tough journey, and that is why most of the morning and evening prayers prescribed by the Prophet SAW are focused on seeking Allah's assistance against our animal self and the whispers of Satan. For example, one of the regular mornings and evening payers of the Prophet SAW include:

(O Ever Living, O Self-Subsisting and Supporter of all, by your mercy I seek assistance, rectify for me all of my affairs and do not leave me to myself, even for the blink of an eye).

There are certain times in your life that lend themselves to change and that make change quicker and deeper. These include marital relationship struggles, but we are forgetful.

We always sleepwalk into our daily life until something happens to wake us up, something that rocks us back and makes us ask ourselves the question "Who do you think you are?". This vulnerable state, if we stay present with it, will be the birthplace of joy and belonging. This frees us from adopting a 'victim' stance and from dwelling on and obsessing about the ways we feel we have been wronged.

Complaining about painful, seemingly unfair events without ever considering whether and to what extent we have played a role in them is common. Our inclination to sin is part of our nature. We need to spend a few moments in bed before we sleep and ponder on the mistakes we made during the day. Sometimes we need to go even deeper and look into the wishes behind our spouse's criticism as behind every criticism there is a wish. There are unmet needs and longing and you need to identify those un-met needs behind the wallpaper of your spouse. It easier to figure out these wishes when you gain self-knowledge.

Benefit 2(You Cultivate Good Character)

"When asked about the best of the believers, the Prophet SCW replied, They are those who have the best character and manners."

Life in itself is our greatest teacher and whatever we are doing can be instructive. Marital life though is one of the best institutions for personal growth. There was a saying by Gandhi: *"I first learned the concepts of non- violence in my marriage"*. Similarly, the philosopher Socrates says: *"By all means, marry. If you get a good wife, you'll become happy; if you get a bad one, you'll become a philosopher"*. The marital relationship is a school, a learning environment in which both partners can grow and develop over time.

Character building begins in our infancy and continues until death. It is all about the heart, and the heart cannot be taught cognitively in the classroom to students mechanically taking notes. Good, wise hearts are developed through lifetimes of diligent effort to dig deeply within and heal a lifetime of scars. It has to be discovered within the depths of your own soul, and the marital journey helps you to do this.

It is hard at the beginning, when couples enter a period of adjusting to each other. This is because every husband or wife brings behaviors, beliefs and roles into their marriage that they are not even aware of. Like an actor in a dramatic performance following a script (the one we observed growing up), each of us plays a part in our marriage to which we haven't given much thought. A wife, describing her character development in her marriage, stated: "I keep falling in love with the same man, over and over again.

The reason being that he keeps changing, I keep changing and we are both developing. The process continues, and every so often we realise that each of us is so much more than the man or woman whom we married. When I first married, I thought I knew all about him, but as time went on and we grew up together, I found in him new colours and qualities of character; it's quite exciting." It is in relationships that we learn to be unselfish and loving. And no relationship has a greater impact on your life than marriage, if you get married.

A well-handled marital conflict strengthens your character; this does not happen overnight but gradually over a long time, in small steps. It's important to cultivate an appreciation for the small improvements when they happen. Success builds upon itself, and slowly, it lays down a permanent route to change. Every moment in marital life has the possibility of delighting us, nurturing us, supporting us, if we are here to see it.

Ralph Waldo Emerson put it well:

"Sow a thought and you reap an action; sow an act and you reap a habit; sow a habit and you reap a character; sow a character and you reap a destiny."

The longevity of your marital life is determined by the thoughts you sow and your awareness of your thoughts. The Prophet Muhammed (SAW) said you must focus on the positive aspects of your spouse, as this approach helps you acknowledge your partner. This will in turn increase the level of love and respect between you. By also making a habit of viewing issues with a 'glass half full' approach, your character strengthens.

It is liberating for you and the people around you. Your creativity level will be very high, as you will save all those energies you would have consumed on negativity. Negativity consumes our lives, but if we succeed in liberating ourselves from it, we will reap a fruitful reward in our marital and social lives, and life will be more meaningful.

Below is summary of positive lessons we learn:

- **Controlling the tongue**

Although we know it to be true, the genuine realisation of the importance of controlling the tongue happens in our marital life. Let us not forget that this is one of the most important prescriptions the Prophet SAW gave us. Through marital experience, we see in practice how we misuse our words so often, and the way this misuse leads us to pull each other down and keep each other in a state of fear and doubt.

The following quote makes good sense: *"A slip of the tongue leads to a slip of the mind, which leads to a slip of the soul"*. Something slips out of our mouths and, because of pride, must be rationalized and justified (the "slip of the mind"). That very denial of our original mistake leads to our "slip of the soul." One little piece of misinformation or miscommunication can break down communication between the entire family, causing everyone it touches to be contagious to others.

This mistake happens when we are in a reactive state of mind, especially when we are overwhelmed, stressed and tired. But with realisation comes transformation, and that is when we can fully implement the three principles of "Listen before you answer", "Think before you speak" and "Let your heart instruct your tongue."

- **Not taking things personally:**

Marriage teaches us that we are different from each other, and we start putting our self in the other person's shoes. But at the beginning, we assume everyone knows what is in our world, and we try to impose our world on their world. When you take things personally, you feel offended, and your reaction is to defend your beliefs and create conflict. As time goes on, we are able to cultivate a solid habit of not taking anything personally. We learn that whatever someone thinks is simply the way they see the world and is nothing personal. This allows us to avoid many upsets in our life.

- **Not jumping to conclusions**

This means not making assumptions. In our experience of marital life, we usually start making assumptions, we misunderstand and we end up creating a whole big drama for nothing. We assume that our partners know what we think and that we don't have to say what we want.

After a lot of difficulties and misunderstandings, we begin to appreciate the importance of asking for clarification. This means that our relationship stops suffering from conflicts created by mistaken assumptions. We need to avoid building 'relationship roadblocks' out of these assumptions.

This allows you to recover all the energy that you invested in making assumptions. You can then use all that energy for your lifelong dream of "Marital Tranquility" promised in the Quran by Allah. This act is a continuous practice that both willing married partners go through.

Our minds are brilliant, but also stubborn, and habits become ingrained. But through repetition, couples can master how to pay attention to when they are making assumptions, and to recognise that they are assumptions in the first place. There are many periods of transition in the marital relationship where making assumptions are frequent. These include pregnancy, the introduction of a child, moving home, changing jobs and illness in one of the partners.

These life-changing challenges teach us how to make allowances for them and gracefully adjust to the next step in the process. If we are mindful of these challenges, we have a better chance of becoming more loving and happier. Hope keeps love alive. Stop hoping and the marriage dies. As long as we imagine a better marriage and keep believing that we are going to one day enjoy it, the battle against bad things can still be won.

To sum up, it is Allah's way to use trials to test your character. Exercising patience during tough times in your marital life, or indeed in other aspects of your life, will strengthen your character. It is your ability to go through tests and still remain resilient. This is not a gift you are born with. It is like a muscle; the only way you build a muscle is by stressing it. Your muscle does not grow unless it is strained, stretched and stressed. This is the only way to build a character and achieve a solid moral core that leads to self-respect and inner triumphs.

Having or attaining self-respect is not the same as self-confidence or self-esteem. It is not based on IQ, not comparative and not earned by being better than other people at something. It is earned by being better than you used to be, by being dependable in times of testing, straight in times of temptation. It can only be earned by a person who has endured some internal temptation who has confronted their own weakness.

Such character development enables you to turn the Whole thing around in a conflict. Shifting it from negative escalation to reflective listening or from reacting to reflecting. You will become not only a peace maker in your marriage, but in your community and country. Those who write about Abraham Lincoln, acknowledge that he has cultivated his patience, tolerance and forgiveness from navigating well through a tough marriage. There is no pain free relationship.

Finally, for good character development to manifest itself takes time and energy. This is highly overlooked in our today's culture of immediacy. We need to seriously change the myth of overnight success. The flower doesn't go from bud to blossom at once and yet, as a culture, we ignore the journey of the character blossoming. But that's where all the real magic unfolds in the making of one's character and destiny.

Benefit Three "Love Level Goes up"

From "Being loved" to "Loving"

After the couple resolve their issues or conflict constructively, there will be a growing realisation that "Happily Ever After" doesn't exist. Every day you wake up and decide to love your partner and your life in the good times, the bad and the ugly. Some days, it's a struggle and some days you feel like the luckiest person in the world. We realise that real love requires self-discipline and a certain amount of sustained effort over the course of years and lifetime. This realisation is vital for the relationship to grow on a higher level after the "In-Love" honeymoon period ends.

This period is delusional and full of fantasies, as each person in the couple is in for the feelings, and the feelings run out if the marriage is not maintained well. This however does not mean that you should wish for or seek marital conflict; one must pray not to have it. But if it occurs, one must embrace it. Always remember, *"Out of suffering have emerged the strongest souls; the most massive characters are seared with scars."*

It is a fact that when couples constructively resolve their marital conflicts in the spirit of love and unity, everyone feels that was the moment they have truly lived. Our negative attitude towards the relationship changes, and that is the key to marital contentment. It must be acknowledged that relationships are by nature difficult, because people are difficult by nature. If life was just all fun, then nothing good would ever get done. No one would ever grow and settle into the mystical land of a relationship where each person is accepted unconditionally for whoever he or she is, without expectation.

When couples navigate through their conflict successfully, they move from a state of "Being loved" to "Loving". The problem with simply "being loved" is that it is unsustainable in adult life. It may work in childhood as your parent is simply spontaneously on hand to comfort, guide, entertain, feed, clear up, and remain almost always warm and cheerful. Parents don't reveal how often they've bitten their tongue, fought back the tears or been too tired to take off their clothes after a day of childcare. The relationship is almost always entirely non-reciprocal; the parent loves but they don't expect the favour to be returned.

This is why in adulthood when we first say we 'long for love', what we predominantly mean is that we want to be loved as we were once loved by a parent; we want this love to be recreated. This is a disaster for any relationship, and this is what pushes couples to move firmly out of the childhood mentality and into the parental position. Each person becomes someone who can sometimes subordinate their own demands to the needs of another in order to be an adult in love.

They reach the true mature love of at least putting someone else's needs ahead of your own. The love level grows because couples start to look at the marriage from the perspective of a glass half full or look at the flower from the branch and not the thorn. They tend to focus the best in their mate and appreciate each other. This is in line with the prescription given by Prophet Muhammad SAW in looking at the good side of your mate.

I remember my Grandma describing her marriage in this way: "I already knew our 'ever after' wouldn't always be happy or even comfortable and clearly it couldn't be expected to go according to plan. Still, it was *ours* and we were both determined enough to see it through to the end." Real love teaches us the courage to face up to and rise above the challenges life brings. When love is at this stage couples are able to see beyond words spoken out of pain, and instead see a person's soul. It is when you've been with someone for years, cared for them when they're ill, put up with them when they're grumpy, taken the sharp side of their tongue and still come back.

It is when you've acted quite appallingly, and the other person still accepts you. They become a catalyst for your soul. You do not need them in order to exist, but you desperately need them in order to be a better *you*. The struggle against the weakness in your self is never a solitary struggle. There are also couples who do not see growth in their marital love, and one of the reasons could be that their relationships are conditional in nature.

The problem with conditional relationships is that they implicitly prioritise something else above the relationship. So, it's not *you* I really care about, but rather your wealth or beauty. It often causes you to feel one thing about a person and show them something completely different. Conditional relationships are all smoke and mirrors where you never actually know who the other person is. Many people enter into a marital relationship as a way to compensate for something they lack or hate within themselves. This is a one-way ticket to an unhealthy relationship because it means your love is conditional.

I witnessed incidents like this in Somalia after the Civil war. There were many cases where someone married for the wealth or political position of the other's family. The civil war caused many rich people to lose their wealth and political status; we have witnessed many couples abandoning one another. Because the conditions that were binding them together were gone. Some of us develop the attitude of 'conditional relationships' during childhood, especially if our parents only approved of us when we obeyed their orders, or only liked us when we were achieving good grades.

The only way to short circuit this is to let go of your own conditions and stop accepting other people's conditions. This is the greatest kind of love, and it is love for the sake of Allah/God and this can never diminish as Allah himself is the ever-existing, the ever-living. This is due to the fact that love itself can only exist as long as the reason to love exists. For example, a man in love with the beauty of his wife will only love her as long as her beauty remains. If she loses her beauty due to old age or any other reason, his love for her diminishes.

To love your spouse simply for the sake of loving them is no good, because eventually, the love you have for them will consume you in a way that is completely unhealthy for you, emotionally and spiritually. Below is statement from a husband acknowledging the unconditional love his wife gives him:

"I felt very loved by her, and I loved her intensely too, and this was a love without ambivalence, without conditionality. Nothing I could say could repel or shock her; there seemed no limit to her powers of sympathy and understanding, the generosity and spaciousness of her heart"

Apart from that, most people agree about the joy it brings when couples resolve their disagreement and resume their tranquil life. People describe this in different ways, and some cannot put it into words, but if we look back upon our lives those are the moments when we have truly lived. It is as if the honeymoon period is reborn, and it makes you forget all the psychological pains you went through. One of the main reasons is that couples realise how interdependent we are as humans.

We begin to realise the efforts each one has put in the marriage and how life is without each other. This time you do not fall in love, but you grow *into* love and love grows *in* you. You give your spouse the time to mature and develop to go wrong, to wander in another direction and not to shout at them but to give them every chance to grow at their own pace towards their better selves. Loving deeply doesn't mean wanting to be together every minute. Space is needed to re-ignite your desire for them.   Give love as one is never wounded by the love one gives, only by the love one expects.

Benefit Four: "You learn the behavior of others"

"The best way to judge people is by their own principles, not by your own"

During the wedding ceremony all the family members of the new couple dance and express joy. At that moment, it is difficult to know who is a real friend and who is a foe. The only time you will know the true character or behavior of other people is during difficult periods in your marriage. "A best friend is the only one who walks into your life when the rest of the world has walked out." People always cherish those who help to relieve the gloom of their dark hours more than those who are simply ready to enjoy life with them during times of prosperity.

Knowing the different kinds of people and personality types among your partner's relatives is an effective approach to personal growth. It allows you to understand yourself and the world around you. You will learn that each of us has unique capacities and each has different limitations. You will learn their view of the world, how they react to people and respond to stress. Some do crumble and some are consistent and dependable.

You get surprised sometimes to see your mother in law (out of anger) telling you, "I want you to divorce my daughter now" without listening your side of the story. An hour or a day later, you see her working on your reconciliation. During difficult times in our marriage, we discover why our fiercest rivalries are with those who are closest to us. This is more painful than when you are hurt by someone else. Because they know all the buttons to press even if what they are saying about you is not true. This awareness will give you far more compassion and understanding for others.

As social beings, we are programmed to compare ourselves to others, to our siblings, our neighbours and friends. Such comparison comes into two directions, up and down. Comparing our self to our previous self is the safest and best form of comparison than comparing it with others. Such awareness allows us to successfully navigate our social world and lead us to find the right balance between cooperation and competition.

We become good at figuring other people's behaviours and attitudes. This gives us the benefit of understanding people's needs well enough to know how to cooperate with them and identifying the troublesome members so that we can keep an eye on them. It guides our behaviour, which is the thing we can most control. "A person's character is judged not only by the company they keep but also by the company they avoid." Such exploration of different personalities will equip you to become a better counselor or negotiator.

You will realise that what is good advice for one person can be disastrous for another. You will also realise that personalities are relatively stable and are not going to change depending on the people you come in contact with. *We are who we are.* On the other hand, we learn that attitudes are subject to change. We want to change attitudes because attitudes influence behaviour.

There is a saying, "take advice from a patient who experienced the disease rather than the doctor". In resolving marital conflict, this is a valid statement. For example, if the marital therapist is not married, or if they have been divorced many times or is unhappily married, they do not have the kind of relationship you want and cannot tell you how to achieve it. But the chances of success are higher when you get an advice from someone who has constructively navigated through a difficult marriage and turned it into a happy one. They will help you turn towards one another instead of "turning away".

These are the people to talk to and regard as mentors. Being around negative people is bad for you. One valuable lesson I learnt from my marriage is the danger of harsh criticism. It wounds a person's precious pride, hurts their sense of themselves, and arouses resentment. Most of the time, in retaliation, the person we are going to criticise and condemn, comes back to justify himself or herself. It comes like a thunderstorm if the person was supressing their agony.

Criticism demoralises family members, friends, and work colleagues and yet does not improve the situation that has been criticised. It doesn't lead to lasting changes. Indeed, it makes matters worse and often creates resentment. This taught me to improve myself and strengthened my character by exercising self-control and be understanding and forgiving. By navigating through marital conflict, we become aware of how outside influences affect our relationship. You will know the toxic people in your marital life that display negativity such as gossiping. This will allow you to limit how much time you spend with them.

You will be careful with how much personal information you tell them. You will figure out any person who drains you often, or you feel limits you from being a better person. By figuring it out, you will create healthy boundaries. Sometimes you have to guard your marriage with everything you got. When you are around with good people, you copy and absorb some of their best traits like smelling good perfume odour.

However, it is not advisable to define people according to the known personality traits alone. This type of pigeon-holing people's character may sometimes betray us. It is easier to see who you are or who they are according to one's deeds especially during the difficult times. That is when the real characters are revealed and that is the time your deeds speak louder than your disposition. Such times are not only confined to marital conflict, it could be traveling with people or money issues in business partnership or family inheritance issues.

Finally, dealing with those people around your marital relations will teach you the main principle of "The only way to get out the best of an argument is to avoid it". A misunderstanding is never ended by argument but by tact, diplomacy, conciliation and a sympathetic desire to see the other person's viewpoint. Most of the time, an argument ends with each of the contestants more firmly convinced than ever that he/she is absolutely right. The best way to judge people is by their own principles, not by your own.

Chapter 3

"Character traits that lead to Marital Tranquillity"

"Allah has promised Mawadah/Marital Tranquillity in the Quran, but we need to take the necessary steps to attain it"

1. Expressing Your Love to your spouse

"The deepest urge in human nature is the desire to be valued"

The deepest urge in human nature is "the desire to be valued". Psychologists say it is as almost as deep as the desire for food or sleep. It is human nature to crave to be appreciated and managing to satisfy this need will have a strong positive influence on people in your life such as your spouse, friends and work colleagues. Appreciation and encouragement inspire enthusiasm among people and develop the best in them.

We nourish our bodies with food, but often fall short in nourishing the self-esteem of our spouse, children, neighbours and work colleagues. Showing sincere appreciation can change a person's life. For example, a wife has one driving need: to feel loved, and when that need is met, she is happy. When her spirit deflates during a conflict, she is feeling unloved and the husband feels disrespected.

When a husband chooses to do or say something loving, he energises his wife in a positive way. Similarly, when she expresses herself respectfully, she energises him too. Therefore, you are the only one in the world who can meet your spouse's deepest need for love and respect in marriage. After all, you alone are married to your spouse. The problem is when we lose track of our consistency in expressing our love to our spouse. This drives the relationship into a downward spiral, and even to the point of no return.

Below is a description of a real story from *"short stories of Victorian Troubled Marriage"* by Rudyard Kipling.

Short Stories of Victorian Troubled Marriages

In the daytime, when she moved about me,
In the night, when she was sleeping at my side,--
I was wearied; I was wearied of her presence,
Day by day and night by night I grew to hate her-
Would God that she or I had died!
CONFESSIONS "THE BRONCKHORST DIVORCE-CASE"

Today there are many homes like this that are running on an empty 'love tank'. This would not have happened had we fuelled our home with love. Such need for love and desire is very high on the environment we live in our modern world today. As love is the desire of being desired", today we are struggling to become and remain desirable. Couples expect more from one another and the way forward is to love with tenderness. To be tender is to accept loved one's weaknesses and there is plenty of happiness in tenderness.

The Prophet SAW was very good at this and remains the best role model in every aspect of life. Aisha "Ummul Mu'miniin" once asked him how he would describe his love for her. The Prophet Muhammad (SAW) answered, *"Like a strong binding knot." The more you tug, the stronger it gets, in other words.* Every so often 'Aisha would playfully ask, *"How is the knot?"* The Prophet (SAW) would answer, *"As strong as the first day (you asked)."* Such assurances of love from spouses bring forth feelings of warmth and connection.

Our perspective is enhanced, and we become more satisfied. Most of our homes are empty of this Sunnah of expressing our love in affirming words. Most of us are overcome by shyness and tradition. We assume that our spouse knows that we love them, or we believe that there is no need to show it. Some accept the traditional belief that if you inform your spouse of your love for them, they become controlling. The truth is that when we receive affirming words, we are more likely to be motivated to reciprocate and do something our spouse desires.

The tongue has the power of life and death; use it to keep the love alive in your marriage. Your words have to be sincere expressions of love, not flattery. Flattery is insincere appreciation; it is selfish, superficial, and is universally condemned. On the other hand, sincere expressions of love and appreciation come from the heart, are unselfish and are universally admired. It is the difference between genuine and counterfeit money. The counterfeit money will eventually get you into trouble if you pass it on to someone else.

The purpose of love is not to get something you want, but to do something for the wellbeing of the one you love. To achieve that kind of genuine love requires energy and discipline. Verbal flattery in order to get your spouse to do something that you want may even lead him or her to react angrily. This may be particularly true of those spouses who experienced painful childhood experiences, leading to fear of abandonment and feelings of loneliness related to the past. We must use kind words and say them with tenderness.

Sometimes our words say one thing, but our tone of voice says another. Our spouse will usually interpret our message based on our tone of voice, not the words we use. "You can never say anything but what you are". Showing sincere appreciation and love can change your spouse's life. People are social beings, and hunger for appreciation. It is the currency that all souls enjoy. All of us have areas in which we feel insecure. We lack courage and this hinders us from accomplishing the positive things we want to do.

A loving husband or wife with their encouraging words can act as an important catalyst for change. You need to see something in your spouse that is worth loving and tell your spouse things you like about her/him, things that make you happy. Love need not evaporate after the honeymoon period ends. We can keep it alive by putting more effort into loving each other without the euphoria and obsession of the first one or two years of the marriage, i.e. from the experience of being 'in love' to 'real love'.

Real love means the accumulation of the little good things you said or did for your spouse with sincerity. The problem is lack of consistency; we start to take our spouse for granted and say "She/He knows that I love her/him". We need love as long as we live; we are the human species (social animals). One way of keeping love alive is never forgetting to give your spouse an honest, gentle kiss when you arrive home and when you leave, even if you have some issues between you. This shows that the marriage means a lot to you, and trust emerges as a result.

A study carried out by Dr Chapman during his thirty years of marriage counselling concluded that there many ways you can express your love for your spouse and pooled them into five categories. In his popular book "Five Love Languages" he explains the five ways in detail with great stories. When you read about the prophet Muhammed SAW, you will notice that he practised eloquently all the love languages in his marital life. His words always reconciled with his actions.

Below are the 5 Love languages Dr Chapman stated in his book:

- Words of Affirmation: Saying "I Love you" and similar terms with sincerity
- Quality Time: Sitting together, having deep conversation etc.
- Receiving gifts: Give gifts to another, so you may love one another.
- Acts of service: Helping with the housework etc.
- Physical Touch: Holding hands, kissing and making love.

To love without knowing how to love is dangerous and wounds the person we love. To love is to be kind and this is fighting a hard battle. It requires constant nurturing and attentiveness, it is constant work towards a better tomorrow for you and the other and once one stops it immediately starts decaying. Expressing your love for yourself allows you to learn more about yourself. This lets your spouse know and acknowledge that you did not use the word "Darling" lightly.

2. The Importance of Respecting One Another

The less Respect there are, the more the likelihood of not feeling at home in your home

Respect fuels and revitalises love between people. Respecting the feelings of others, including your spouse, might mean nothing to you but it could mean everything to them. Even though both men and women value respect, to a man, it means even more, and leads him to unconditionally love his wife. We all need respect equally, but there is a felt need in a wife for love and in husband for respect. Unconditional respect is as powerful for him as unconditional love is for her. Both love and respect are like oxygen to a suffocating person and vital to marital longevity.

One of the Prophet Mohamed's (SAW) saying is *"If I were to order anyone to prostrate to someone else other than Allah, I would have ordered the wife to prostrate to her husband* [Ahmad & Ibn Maajah]. The Prophet SCW did not mean to belittle women or the wife, but to emphasise the positive outcome it will generate for the wife in this life and hereafter. When you touch your husband's deepest need for respect, something good almost always happens. This fuels him to express, demonstrate and meet your heartfelt desire for unconditional love.

This in return positively energises the wife and makes the home more peaceful. A study carried out by Dr Emerson involving 7,000 people asked the question; *"During a conflict with your spouse, do you feel unloved or disrespected?"* Results showed that 83% of the men said they feel disrespected and 72% of the women feel unloved. These men were not saying that they are indifferent to love. They need to feel respected even more than to feel loved.

Similarly, women tend to be relationship-oriented, and the deepest question she asks herself quite often is "am I loved?". The more respect and love there are the more immune the marriage will be from negativity. The less there are, the more the likelihood of not feeling at home in your home. Many may argue that "respect should be earned" i.e. "My husband will be respected if he earns it".

This is not the right thought for a marriage to thrive. Your husband might not be worthy of respect, but in marriage you don't marry someone in order to give them what they deserve. In marriage, you give them what you've promised. A husband does not need to earn his wife's respect any more than a wife needs to earn her husband's love. A wife ought to respect her husband because he is her husband, just as he ought to love her because she is his wife. We all seem to understand that love is supposed to be unconditional, but we struggle to see how respect must be the same.

A man must also be respected before he is respectable. Respect normally starts with the wife or with you sister. By giving respect to your husband you are saying to Allah, "Allah I listened to you and obeyed you" and this in itself is a high achievement. As the Prophet (SAW) said *"If a woman dies while her husband is pleased with her, she enters Paradise"*. Respect pleases the husband and it is the one thing they need the most. The problem we are facing today is that the one thing that is consistently withheld from men and husbands is respect, which is the one thing they need the most.

One way to give your husband respect is to give and allow him the leadership role Allah has given him. When you hand over the reins to your husband, you are saying that you need him and you trust him to lead the family, and that you respect that he may do it differently than you but the outcome will be what is best for the family. If you do this wholeheartedly you will notice that your husband tries to please you even more and your respect for him increases. That belief in him, that, he is free to do it his own way and that you have faith and trust in him, makes a man feel like a lion. In return you as an honourable and respectable wife will feel less burdened and will not have the pressure of worrying about everything anymore.

For example, you may feel as if you have to do it all because you don't 'trust' your husband to do it the way you want it to be done or you want it done immediately. This causes an extra burden on you that does not need to be there. It also shows your husband that you do not respect him enough to let him handle the situation. It really does not come down to whether you trust him or if he does it as well as you, it comes down to thinking you know better. This is as if you are indirectly saying to him, *"I don't respect you and I don't trust your judgement."* This makes your husband step back and feel frustrated.

But allowing him the leadership role wholeheartedly will make him grow as a man, a husband, and a father, because you have treated him as a leader in the home long before he had any idea what it meant to lead or how to do it.

Another way to show respect to your husband is to focus on what he does well. Develop an attitude that looks for the best in your husband and responds in ways that build him up. Sometimes without realising it, you may blame your husband for not doing things the way you think they are supposed to be done. You fail to look at your own actions because you are too busy looking at his, and poking holes in them.

Women tend to be controlling of their household especially when they become mothers. They get so caught up in managing their kids that they want to 'manage' their husbands as well. The same is true for the husbands as well. They also have to focus on the good side of their wives. It is admirable to speak well of your husband.

Do not belittle him to your friends or make him feel unnecessary or incapable. Reason being is that you are only on that pedestal because they put you up there. The best thing to do when one is wrong is to educate and not belittle, as that will help the person change their behaviours. Always tell your children the positive aspects of their dad's character, both as a husband and a father. Regularly doing this in front of your spouse not only shows him respect, but also helps the kids develop a loving, respectful attitude towards Dad and the marriage.

Get his input on big decisions. Tell him "this is my opinion, but I leave you to decide". This will lift him up, and he will very likely support your idea. Respect should not be based on his performance. Instead, you should honour him because it pleases Allah. Respect him for who he is, not for what he does. Hold him in high esteem and lift him up and this will make him try to please you more and more and your respect for him will increase.

This however doesn't mean that a man has a license to be lazy, abusive, or uncaring, or that women should tolerate a man who fails in *his* duties. Precisely the opposite, he is challenged to live up to the respect his wife has for him. All in all, hold him in high esteem and lift him up and this is what husbands crave from you. Similarly, to my brothers while you need to hear "I respect you", my sisters want to hear "I Love you".

3. The importance of thanking (Gratitude)

"What is rewarded gets repeated".

"He who does not thank people (for their favours) has not thanked Allah."

Gratitude is the healthiest of all human emotions and the problem we have today is that few people express it. Feeling gratitude and not expressing it is like wrapping a present and not giving it. Allah says in the Quran, **"Few of My servants are grateful"**. Also, Satan acknowledged the importance and value of showing gratitude and swore by saying to Allah, *"You will not find the majority of them as thankful ones"*.

This is an area Satan uses to destroy marriages. If you notice those whispers in your mind that say to you, "you do not need to thank them for this, it is their duty", it is from Satan and you need to seek refuge from satanic whispers.

However, the human mind naturally overemphasizes the negative. Psychologists have found that the loss of something is much more painful than the joy of gaining the same thing. It is why negative news sells better and gets reported and spread so much more readily. It's why we can't turn away from a car accident or two people fighting. It's why it's so much more tempting to relate to others by complaining and gossiping rather than through gratitude. This isn't to say one must ignore what's wrong with the world. But, when things seem bad, don't forget what's good, true and beautiful. It is worthwhile to have a 'glass half full' approach to marital issues.

This form of gratitude is a vital skill in achieving marital happiness. For example, there was a husband who felt withdrawn from his marriage. His father noticed it and asked why he was unresponsive to his wife; his answer was that she had stopped beautifying herself.

The father called his daughter-in-law and explained to his son's complaints. The wife's response was that she very often took care of her appearance, but had received not a single compliment or word of praise from him, and had therefore assumed that he did not care whether she looked good or not. The father apologised to his daughter-in-law and started lecturing his son about the importance of genuine praise, compliments and admiration in marriage. He said women need and like to hear detailed compliments; "you look good" is not enough, you need to go a bit further. For example, "that dress suits you and its colour brings out all your beauty," or "this food is delicious, healthy and the spices are well balanced." Thank her for all the things she did in the house and with the kids. We forget that women have egos, same as men. The outbursts of a woman is because of a blow to her ego that triggered her defence systems.

Ego is also the reason why women are competitive with other women. Because of their egos (and thousands of years of evolution) they are fuelled them to be the most dynamic, attractive and capable female in the room. It is also another reason why they feel the need to control their husbands' lives outside of the relationship. Because of their egos persuade them to conquer men. We can easily prevent this drama with just few words. The common consensus is that women value compliments on their personality and mannerisms over their physicality, and that occasional compliments are more effective sedatives than expensive presents.

Similarly, women also fall short when it comes to thanking their husbands. You will witness many husbands who have been married for over 20 years, who are longing for their wife say, "thank you for your efforts". Some women feel that it is not necessary, or due to insecurity a woman may think it makes her vulnerable if she does it and lets him know how much she values his efforts.

For example, a wife complimented her husband who was a taxi driver, saying to him as he was getting into the car, "You are irreplaceable, drive safely". According to the husband, this simple statement kept him motivated for many years. This enabled him to be cheerful to his passengers, his tips and income consequently went up, and his love for his wife increased. Sincere compliments cost nothing and can accomplish so much. **"What is rewarded gets repeated"**. If you compliment your spouse on something, it is highly likely s/he will do it more.

Dr John Gottman, marriage researcher, states that in good marriages, compliments need to outnumber criticisms by at least five to one. Compliments are the solution to making your spouse feel confident and secure. Dr Laura Trice came to the same conclusion as a result of observing of people who are facing life and death with drug addiction in a rehabilitation clinic.

She found that the core wound of some of the patients comes down to something as simple as "their father died without ever saying he was proud of them". Probably the father did not know his child needed to hear it. Therefore, it is equally important as a parent to thank and admire our children and this should not be under-estimated. Tell your daughter how beautiful she is before someone else tells her. The love of family and the admiration of friends are much more important than wealth and privilege. It is important that your compliments are sincere and honest.

4. <u>Understanding the difference Between Men and Women</u>

One of the main phrases used when couples argue is: "You don't understand me at all, you don't get me, do you?" and to be fair neither one of them is wrong. But both of them are very different, in terms of how they behave and think. We often fail to recognise the differences in the way God designed men and women. Differences that he intended for good and we don't know they exist, or we don't see them as legitimate.

Men and Woman are equal in the sight of God, but this does not mean that we are the same in every aspect. One key to a great marriage is to work with His design rather than against it. That doesn't mean one is better than the other, just that they are unique. Couples complement one another in their differences; they bring different skills and perspectives to the table, and shoulder different burdens in different ways.

In one study, carried out by social researcher Shounti Feldhahn (who herself initially struggled in her marriage), she concluded that men and woman have different insecurities and different ways of communicating. She found that:

The doubt that lives inside most women (about 80 percent) sounds like this: *Am I loveable? Am I special? Would he choose me again?* **This insecurity asks:** *Am I worthy of being loved for who I am on the inside?*

Whereas the doubt that lives inside most men (about 75 percent) sounds quite different: Am I able? Am I adequate? I want to be a great husband (or father or businessman), but am I? This insecurity asks: Am I any good at what I do on the outside?

Because these insecurities are like raw nerves, husbands and wives can unintentionally cause pain to each other. Marital failures sometimes happen these days because we're so obsessed with equality and so averse to things like duty, responsibility, sacrifice, and service.

For example, a man driving his child to school and his wife sitting in the car. He drives through the traffic lights as they are turning from amber to red. The wife tells him that he is irresponsible and does not value her and their son's life. The father feels inadequate, even though by his calculation there was no danger in driving the lights on amber. His main focus was that his son should be on time for school.

Another example: a man buys a gym membership card for his wife as a gift to please her. But she takes it as an insult as if he is telling her she is no longer attractive and gets angry at her husband. When we look at both cases, neither of those feelings is accurate, but they still hurt. Also, the spouse causing the pain often doesn't understand why such a "little thing" would bother his or her mate. There is a need to open our heart and broaden our prospective in order to enhance our marital life. Become aware of these sensitive areas, we will know how to avoid hurting our spouse.

Another issue today is that there are a lot of people who misunderstand or misinterpret Prophet Muhammed's (SCW) saying of; *Treat women kindly, Women has been created from a rib and the most bent part of the rip is the uppermost. If you try to turn it straight, you will break it. And if you leave it alone, it will remain bent as it is. So, treat women kindly. (Al-Bukhari and Muslim).*

The Prophet (SAW) in this hadith was emphasising the differences between men and women. He meant that if a man wants to be happy with his wife, he should not attempt to re-shape her character. Rather, he should accept her the way she is and try to be happy by understanding her habits and her personality. Sadly, it was interpreted according to the cultural traditions and bias against women.

Such misinterpretation gained wide circulation and fostered the un-Islamic idea of women's inferiority. Another dangerous issue that makes our marriages fall apart is that many of us have been raised on the lie of marital and gender "equality." We have been told that there is no difference between a husband and a wife, the two are interchangeable, exactly the same in every way that matters, and so they approach the marriage with the expectation that they're marrying mirror images of themselves. As a result, we have become obsessed with equality and averse to things like duty, responsibility, sacrifice, and service. Such aversion leads to a cycle of negativity at home.

But a marriage that has no concern for equality and, instead, is fuelled by the sacrificial love of both spouses, is the kind of marriage that will survive while so many others collapse around them in a cloud of immaturity and selfishness. Such selfishness makes people like your spouse turn into an object for the purpose of providing you love.

Therefore, we need to make serious changes or sacrifices in our new life as a married couple in order to sail through the choppy waters of our marital life. We need to work with male/female differences, rather than against them; if we do so, we can definitely help couples live happily in many areas of married life. Remember, one statement or sentence might mean one thing to you and another to your wife and husband.

For example: "I have nothing to wear" might be expressed differently by both husband and wife. For him to mean "I have nothing clean to wear" and for her "I have nothing new to wear".

Above all, we need to understand each other's purposes in order to achieve a harmonious relationship. Allah has created men and women with perfectly complementary designs. It is when husband and wife expect each other to think, react, and behave in the same ways and not appreciate their God-given differences that they experience conflict.

It is important to understand that your needs are different from each other's. For example, if as a wife you want your husband to fulfil his purpose, you must learn his nature, how he functions and what his needs are. You cannot give him what *you* need, as his needs are often different from yours. Below is a summary of some of the differences:

- *Men do not rate feelings as highly in their minds as women, while women don't rate abilities as high as men. For example, men love to have their abilities recognized and appreciated and hate to have them* scorned or ignored. On the other hand, women love to have their feelings recognized and appreciated and hate to have them ignored.

- Men like to solve problems on their own, yet women like to solve problems in the relationship as a team. Men can sometimes view unsolicited assistance as an undermining of their effort to solve problems alone while women value assistance, and thus view unsolicited solutions as undermining their effort to proceed interactively. Men want their solutions to be appreciated; women want their assistance to be appreciated and this creates misunderstandings.

- Men emotionally detach themselves when they fear that their self-sufficiency is threatened. At these times, they become unapproachable, withdrawn and demand they be left alone and be allowed to not express their feelings. But if they are given support in the form of space, they soon feel better and spring back into their usual selves. It can be frustrating for women to handle the harshness with which men retreat and then subsequently spring back.

- *Women will also from time to time emotionally sink into themselves. They may become negative and start to dwell on every problem which troubles them, including ones which have already been raised and solved before. Plus, if they cannot find any real issues to concentrate on, then they will find some random other thing to worry about. If women are supported and allowed enough time to express and release their negative feelings, they will start to feel happy again and return to their usual selves. This slowness may be hard for men to handle.*

We need to recognize these differences and that everyone needs time and space from time to time, however, our partner only wants to help because he/she cares. Do not fault them for trying to be there for you. It takes a courage to give space to the other when all you want is closeness. And yet this difficult act may be the very thing that saves the relationship over and over. It is true "Sometimes, the best thing is said not when we exchange words, we just exchange space".

Understanding Sexual needs of Husband and Wife

Sex is still a big taboo topic among Muslims, even in the West. We cannot talk or raise questions as it is considered something filthy and evil. Obviously, we all know that Islam prohibits having sex outside of marriage. But for a lawful marriage we need to educate ourselves about Islamic bed manners. The first generations of Muslims or the Sahabah never shied away from seeking the answer to intimate questions. We should not feel embarrassed when sexual desires are completely normal and natural feelings for a human being to have, and there is nothing wrong with fulfilling them in the halal way.

Many of us are introduced to sex via friends, movies and television, internet, books and biology class. But none of these describes well the emotional, psychological and spiritual aspects of sex. As a result, many people experience sexual frustration because they have developed wrong ideas and unrealistic expectations from watching movies and television. The manner today's media depicts sexuality is often false, full of fantasy and destructive to real relationships.

For instance, pornographic images are especially dangerous because they often become imprinted on people's minds and can be a spiritual stronghold. It will be difficult to pray your Salaat and do good deed as the mind is full of these images. Most of us suffer from the consequences of an ill-informed or unwise attitude to sexual activity. Much of what we have learned about sex has been acquired within an unwholesome context and is filled with misinformation. According to sex therapists, most of us act like we are performers in someone else's script. We demand our bodies to look and act the part, we pretend we're feeling things that we are not, we ignore emotions and things that we want to say, we ignore our instincts - all in the name of what we think sex is supposed to be. The problem is we are missing ourselves on our sex life. We have begun to look outside of ourselves and look to the world to tell us what sex is. As a result, we walk around thinking there's something wrong with us, taking it personally, wondering what we're missing and thinking we don't measure up. Nothing could be further from the truth. We have put ourselves and sex in a box that is simply way too small, and like anything that gets put in a cage, it and we want to be free. Sex is bigger than that and it is spiritual journey if carried out in Halal way.

It shows us parts of ourselves we've never seen before. It is an adventure, a hidden landscape and an open horizon that is waiting for us every single time. It depends entirely on us being ourselves. Because sex is not about knowing what we're doing; it is about knowing what we're feeling and learning to trust that. So how do we get here? We start by trusting three things: the reality of our bodies, the role of our emotions and the wisdom of our pleasure.

Our sexual bodies are so much bigger than we give them credit for. We, all of us, this entire body, this is our sexual landscape, and we often rush past it as if sex was only about the genitals. We need to open up and include our definition of sex everything that was actually happening. We need to stop our definition of what sex, pleasure and orgasm is. Our hearts and our bodies are intimately connected. The problem is we've come up with the idea that sex and emotion don't belong in the same room together, and when they end up there, there's a problem.

Our emotions are incredible messengers and textures that rise up to give us information, to guide us, to tell us what we're longing for, to tell us what we need, what we want to give and receive. They are a part of our sexual experience, and if we hold back our emotions, our bodies will hold back pleasure - and our capacity for connection. Sex is a revolution that will travel from body to body, from breath to breath, and touch to touch. Sex doesn't start in the bedroom; it starts before we even begin touching. It is how we relate to ourselves and how we emotionally connect to our partners.

According to Sarah Byrden, who has done extensive research how the media misinterpret sex states that "Sex is not a place for us to know. It is a place for us to come alive and discover. And in the end, we hold the keys to this cage. Sex, like any endangered species, is depending on us to save it. Instead of focusing on sex as a performance, Bryden recommends looking at it as playful. When we look back on the sayings of the Prophet Muhammed SAW, he used to use the word "play" when talking about couples making love, as seen in the hadith narrated by *Jabir bin `Abdullah.*

For those who are not married yet, the first night of marriage is a great example. You can easily see in the eyes of young people who are getting married the expression of fear and worry. I was in that situation too and looking back, I wish I had known better. Most of the information you get from people is inaccurate, and your doubts and worries don't let you fully enjoy the happiness of these first intimate moments.

For example, one of the things most people advise you to do is to go straight for the goal. That is a bad idea, and it will seem as if your main objective in marriage is limited to this desire to fulfil your sexual needs. But the goal is way bigger than this. When you contemplate Prophet Muhammed's (SAW) recommendation on the first night, you will clearly see going for the intimacy goal is not a good idea: *"When you enter upon your wife (for the first time), you have first to perform two rak'ats and then hold your wife's head and say, "O Allah! Bless my wife for me, bless me for my wife, give her bounty out of me, and give me bounty out of her!" Then you can do what you want."* [Reported by Abu Dawud]

Most of the Islamic scholars on marital issues recommend taking your time and making both of you feel relaxed and comfortable. They say it is the night to have good real conversation about what each expects from the other.

It is better to come to your wedding night wearing a learner's hat, and the beauty of this is that learners do not have anything to lose but everything to gain. So, prepare to become a student of your spouse, not just on the wedding night, but for the rest of your married life. Beware of Bollywood's and Hollywood's super-high expectations, as this can set you up for serious disappointment when things don't go according to plan. **You don't have to have a perfect wedding night**.

In fact, most couples will tell you that they did not have a picture-perfect wedding night. But they loved it anyway. With all the embarrassments and little issues, it was the start of their married life and they wouldn't trade the experience for anything. There's so much to be grateful for and so much to look forward to. So, don't exchange the joy and fun for perfect. Enjoy it and keep in mind that it's not *all* you have.

There are hundreds of nights to come. Sexual harmony may not be attained in the beginning of the marital life. It is also important to remember that lawful sexual intimacy is not merely the discharge of sexual feelings. It is more than that. Angels are pleased about a man and wife in their relationship. There is tranquillity in it. The sleep that comes after couples have intimacy is so deep and blessing from Allah SWT. Arabs call it "Nowmatul Aruus". It also softens the heart. Imam Ghazali said the central pleasure of marital couple's intimacy is an indication and glimpse of the delight of Aakhirah or hereafter.

Additionally, for most men, sex isn't just a physical need; it's primarily an emotional one. A husband needs to know that his wife desires him. That affirmation gives a man a sense of well-being that carries over into every other area of his life. Conversely, if he feels it's a little too easy for his wife to say, "I'm too tired," he has a depressing sense that he must be undesirable.

However, he can avoid this pain by approaching his wife in the way that she needs. Women need anticipation time and a wife needs to feel close to her husband outside the bedroom. Letting her know in advance what he has on his mind will help her to become physically excited. It is also not acceptable for a husband to abuse his wife physically and verbally and expect to enjoy sexual pleasure with her at night. That enjoyment will not bring any benefits to both of them. The Prophet (SAW) condemned such behaviour and said ""How does any one of you abuse his wife and then sleep with her at night?" (Bukhari).

The Prophet SAW also emphasised the superiority of Caressing One's wife and said in a Hadith: *"Everything that does not pertain to the remembrance of Allah is amusement except the following four things: 1- Caressing one's wife, 2- Taming one's horse, 3- Shooting arrows, 4- Learning how to swim.* Some men are so self-centred that they do not bother caressing. They are only interested in satisfying themselves.

As a matter of fact, women have desire similar to men. However, men tend to orgasm too soon; they should do their best to delay the moment of ejaculation for as long as possible. The more the pleasure the spouse experiences as well, the happier they are. Therefore, when the husband has sexual intercourse with his wife, he should take into consideration that he is required to satisfy his wife too. Women need affection before proceeding.

It is also vital to keep the bedroom secrets of your partner. Telling your partner's bedroom secrets is an immoral act and may damage your relationship. *The Prophet SCW said: "Perhaps a man might discuss what he does with his wife, or perhaps a woman might inform someone what she did with her husband?" The people were silent. Then I said: "O, Yes! O Messenger of Allah verily both the women and men do that." Then the Prophet said: "Do not do that.*

5. Controlling your anger

"Anybody can become angry — that is easy, but to be angry with the right person and to the right degree and at the right time and for the right purpose, and in the right way — that is not within everybody's power and is not easy." Aristotle

Anger is one of the most complex and distinctive of the human emotions as it involves bodily, psychological, social, and moral dimensions, and anger can and ought to be felt and acted upon in a number of right ways. Unfortunately, people often fail to see the long-term consequences of uncontrolled anger.

Those can include health effects, and social disharmony among family members and friends. It is always better and more worthwhile to not let your anger lead to hatred, as you will hurt yourself more than the other person. *"The best fighter is never angry."* If you are patient in one moment of anger, you will escape a hundred days of sorrow.

It's never what people do that makes us angry; it's what we tell ourselves about what they did. The more anger towards the past you carry in your heart, the less capable you are of loving in the present. Therefore, the best approach is to exercise compassion, explain your anger instead of expressing it, and you will find solutions instead of arguments. Always remember that you cannot make others as you wish them to be, since you cannot make yourself as you wish to be. *"The greatest remedy for anger is delay"*.

The Prophet's SAW remedy on anger was that when one of you feels angry, sit down if standing, and lie down if sitting. If the anger still does not abate, wash with cold water or take a bath, as fire cannot be extinguished without water. The reason is that "Anger comes from the devil and the devil is made of fire." Anger is not our enemy, it is merely a tool at our disposal, and like any tool it can be used mindfully or mindlessly.

Imam Al-Ghazali describes anger as:

"A hunting dog that does not oppose the hunter who trained it. Anger is led, like a hunting dog, by the intellect and sacred law, abiding by their guidance".

This is only possible after a great deal of spiritual struggle against the self and becoming habituated to forbearance and resisting those things that cause anger." Taken in this light, we can see that our anger serves us, so long as we do not allow our anger to control us. We need to have anger as there are many situations in life which call for anger, including righting a wrong, ensuring justice is delivered in a court of law, and protecting the rights of orphans and widows, to name a few.

Additionally, to control anger, one must look under the anger at the deeper emotions. When we pull back the layers of anger, we will find that there are numerous other feelings just lying in wait, including guilt, shame, hurt, loss, longing, hunger, anxiety, unworthiness, and emptiness.

Ask yourself: "Am I angry because I'm actually afraid?" Or maybe you're angry because you feel devastated? Maybe you feel angry because you feel dishonoured or ashamed of yourself. In these circumstances, it is your *ego* pushing you to respond. The best reaction is no reaction at all. Jalaladdin Rumi said, "When you see the face of anger, look behind it and you will see the face of pride. Bring anger and pride under your feet, turn them into a ladder and climb higher. There is no peace until you become their master. Let go of anger, it may taste sweet, but it kills.

However, if your anger is coming from a place of worry for the wellbeing of another who is oppressed, or the concern for your own valid rights (your pride is not a right), there are ways to train yourself to express your anger in a healthy manner. In a marital life context, we occasionally vent to let off steam, but what is totally wrong is when we make venting an integral part of our regular communication.

When one person is a regular venter, the other person often feels like a punching bag. One of the problems with venting is that there is an endless supply of material to vent over. In other words, there will always be things to be upset about if your focus is in that direction. Therefore, if you associate feeling better with letting off steam while talking to your spouse, it becomes addictive and easily turns into a habit.

Therefore, the best way to immunise yourself from the negative effects of your mood or your partner's is to wait, to understand that your perspective is being influenced by your mood. When your mood is calm, feel free to discuss, share your dissatisfactions and think about your problems. You will find that in most cases, whatever was bothering you has probably disappeared, or at least seems trivial. In cases where you are still feeling bothered, you will have more wisdom and common sense available to you. It is best to fight when the mood is right. "Freedom is the ability to instantly transform a bad mood into a good one."

By choosing peace over irritation, you will be rewarded with harmony in your relationship. It seems appropriate to act and feel frustrated when something happens that you do not like. But when you look, you will notice you really do have a choice. You have the ability to respond differently, for example being willing to let go of your partner's mistake, and this experience will bring you closer together. "Letting go gives us freedom, and freedom is the only condition for happiness. There is an important distinction to understand, that you cannot completely control your emotions. Emotions of any kind, including anger, do not go away and do not change.

The key is to actually let go of trying to control anger, but let it flow through you. This results in you becoming much simpler and happier. Your emotion or feeling of anger is not as it used to be. It is like "Oh, I am angry right now. But still doing the thing I want to do." Dealing with your partner's anger is a totally different game. You need to help your partner calm down and go through the process mentioned above.

Your part is to be supportive, listen actively and ask clarifying questions. Remind yourself that your partner is coming from his or her perspective and personal experiences. Your own perspective and feelings are not important at this time. It is okay to say when angry and in argument, "Honey let me go and just chill for a second because otherwise I'm going to regret what I'm going say and I don't want to do that."

You can also state to your spouse "you need to not follow me around the house, you need to let me go and trust that I will come back". But bear in mind, the person who leaves has the right to go but they have to be the one to come back. Such delay gives you time to ponder and look at the issue from every prospective. You never know that anger is triggered by something that happened to you in childhood and your spouse hit that button. It is okay to inform him or her how it felt and verbalise your experience, for example saying:

"When I thought about yesterday it brought back something for me that has nothing to do with you. It actually brought me back the time when I was bullied at school, and you made me feel small like that. I felt the same overwhelming emotions, was afraid to explode and ruin your day"

If you are able to do this for your partner, be assured that you will see big, positive changes in your relationship. Also, by keeping up your end of the relationship and focus on being the best partner you can be, your partner will eventually follow and give you the same courtesy when you are upset and need support. *"Don't waste your time in anger, regrets and grudges. Life is too short to be unhappy."* Learn to appreciate the beauty in life, and everything else will fall into place.

6. <u>Live each day as if it were your last</u>

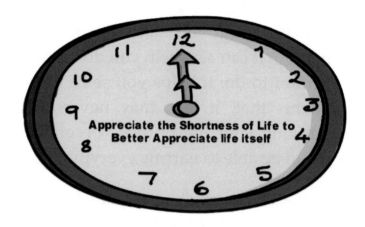

"Treat every moment as your last" as an approach to marital life has a hugely positive impact in life. Because when you think that way, the first thing comes to your mind is being accountable to Allah, leaving and being on good terms with your family. There was observational study done by Mathew O'Reilly who worked on a critical care unit in New York, responding in a number of accidents ranging from car accidents to Hurricane Sandy. The main themes of the last words of the people he was caring for were the need for forgiveness, and regrets. Some of the patients' last words included "I wish I had spent more time with my family".

This approach implies a "do it now" attitude, and this can affect every phase of your life. It can help you do the things you should do but don't feel like doing. But it can also help you do those things that you want to do. It helps you seize those precious moments that, if lost, may never be retrieved. Identifying your life purpose becomes clearer as you will be able to narrow everything down.

Living each day as it were your last leads you to being good to your wife or husband. This is a precious and valuable deed and was strongly emphasised in Prophet Mohamed's last speech in "farewell Hajj". It is difficult to cultivate such an attitude of being present and being 'in the moment' whilst conscious of Allah. But once you master it, life will have more meaning to you and it becomes worthwhile living every moment. This however does not mean that you must live your life as if it is going to end now, and that it is not worth dreaming or having a future to work towards. The real point is to try to utilise the time we have in a meaningful and productive way in achieving well in this world and in the hereafter.

By adopting the idea of "living every moment as your last moment", it makes you become conscious of yourself, your thoughts, behaviour, surroundings and your impact on others. There are many thoughts, both negative and positive, that come to our mind. They are not ours, but we become the ones we listen to or internalise. With a 'last moment' mentality, you are able to figure out the good from the bad thoughts. The anxiety stimulated by the thought of being near to death brings you down to your deep self.

As a spouse or a parent, it makes you much calmer and more patient and less irritable. You will be living with the realisation that today will never re-occur. In this way your only opportunity will be to do what you can today. And how you can make sure, in the craziness of day-to-day life, to stop and appreciate those you love and acknowledge the blessings that you have with gratitude. For me, the remembrance of the civil war in Somalia, makes me realise how short life is. I have seen many deaths and this made me value every second I breathe. But as time goes by, we tend to forget.

Remembering death does not mean killing all dreams of achieving worldly gains, but leads you to make valuable and fruitful worldly decisions. "It does not matter how long you live, but how well you do it or you live it". That is why you witness many very old farmers planting trees that will take many years to bear fruit even though they may not witness harvest time. The reason is that they are aware that the trees they consumed were planted by other elders who left the world, but their legacy continues until today.

Scholars advise that when it comes to doing your worldly life related duties, it is best at best to carry out "every day as your first day" with a fear of Allah. This allows us to be more creative and fearless, like children who enjoy the moment and are not afraid to try new things and explore. It also makes you more focused, result oriented and this helps you finish your project. But when it is about performing deeds of worship, the quality of it will increase if you perform it as your last day, last hour or last minute. When you do that meeting with Allah will come into your mind.

Let's remember the old Muslim adage, *"Work for your world as if you are going to live forever and work for your hereafter as if you are going to die tomorrow."* Time, after all, is a precious commodity and it the most common gift that Allah ever gave any human. As humans on earth, the only thing that we are given that is common to everyone is time. All of us are different heights, different weights, different colours, different economic strata, different families, different ethnic backgrounds and we are from different cultures, but this is the one thing we all have in common.

This is important because what you are and what you become depends on how you use your time. You and I have the same amount of time. "The most intelligent one from among you is he who remembers death the most, and the most prudent one from among you is he who is the most prepared for it." I recently realised how un-prepared I was, when I had a car accident on our way to Birmingham to attend a charity event. While on M1 motor way, our car was hit by fast running BMW and made 6 times 360 degree round.

Fortunately, all these six times, no cars were coming, otherwise we would have gone by now. When the car stopped and driver put the hazard light on, then we saw cars and Lorries coming. We managed to move the car to the corner and no injuries except the damage of the hit. On that day, this book came into to my mind. I only wrote 30 pages at the time. But, ever since the accident, my focus on my writing increased and procrastination decreased. I am now always grateful for every breath and when I wake up every morning healthy and breathing. I have realised that time is not just money. It is more expensive than gold, diamonds and pearls.

Time is life itself! And "The breaths of man are his steps to death. That is why it is well advised to attend janazah or funeral prayers, as well as visit the graves of those who have made the transition into the hereafter, for these too will serve as reminders of our eventual fate. Therefore, treat everyone such as your spouse fairly and nicely. Remember you are but a bundle of days. As each day passes away, a portion of you vanishes away.

This is how Prophet Muhammad SAW, would plan his day. He would divide his day into three parts: (1) for his family, (2) for spirituality (worship), usually a time in seclusion at night, and (3) for personal and social affairs (the majority of this time would be spent dealing with people's problems, overseeing, educating, and mobilizing his community). He never wasted time and always warned against timewasting. Hassan al Basri, a renowned scholar, once said, "I have lived with a people who were stingier with their time than you people are with your money."

7. The Importance of Saying Sorry

Apologising does not mean
You are wrong and the other person is right
It just means, you value your relationship
More than your ego

One of the greatest skills or strengths in social relations is the ability to see your own flaws and take responsibility for them. In your marriage, misunderstanding and conflict are always part of the package, and you will find yourself having to say, "I am sorry", or having someone say it to you. The problem we have these days is that apologising is undervalued and underused. An apology may not cure all wounds, but it does show that you at least see the need to say, "I am sorry". This indicates that you mean business and the marriage matters to you.

It shows you are mature enough to accept responsibility for what you did wrong. It brings a sense of relief and removes tension. The art of the sincere and heartfelt apology is one of the greatest skills you will ever learn. This demonstrates a higher level of self-awareness and self-control, when you are able to look clearly at the hurt you have caused. This leads you to feel empathy for the hurt party and apologize from an authentic centre.

Sometimes, you withhold an apology for having wronged someone, in a state where you were not yourself. Because some experiences can never be understood by those who have not experienced them. In marital life, genuine apology is the super glue of the relationship. A meaningful apology is one that communicates three R's: regret, responsibility, and remedy. If an apology is followed by an excuse or a justification, it means that it is highly likely you are going to commit the same mistake in the future you just apologised for. The hero isn't the one who is right, but the one who steps forward to take the blame—deserved or not—and apologise to save a relationship."

Apologies require an expression of vulnerability and an acceptance of responsibility; no justifications belong in any apology. Say, "I am sorry, it is my fault" and "what can I do to make it right?". It should not be delayed as the longer you hold onto an apology; the harder it is to give. You can edit what you write. Why not edit what you say? If it hurts somebody, you can still offer an apology or withdraw your statements. The injured party does not want to be compensated because he/she has been wronged; they want to be healed because he/she has been hurt.

The right time to say I'm sorry is when you know that you have done anything to hurt someone else, regardless of whether it was intentional or unintentional. The truth is you did, and you need to take responsibility for what you did. The entire foundation of saying sorry is based on the fact that you acknowledge your mistake. Unless you are sure of what mistake you have committed there is no point in apologising. One of the wrong reasons in apologising is when you are apologising just that the other person will be quiet.

This way you are making a bad situation worse. One of the worst things you can do is put the blame back on other person by saying "Well, I am sorry if you feel this way." Another mistake many people make when apologising is telling the other person "It will never happen again." If it does happen again, you will be seen as a person whose word cannot be trusted. Such a loss of trust destroys the marital relationship. It is best to avoid the word "but", as this changes the entire meaning of your apology. The word "but" will indicate that you are not truly sorry and are instead trying to defend yourself for your act.

Also, avoid passing on responsibility to someone else or involve them in your mistake. Along with apologising to your spouse, it is a good idea to suggest something to make it up to them. Sometimes the damage is such that you need to do something so that they forgive you for your mistake. So, while apologising, be prepared to offer them something to make them feel better. After apologising, give them some space to come out of it. It will take them time to recover from it.

8. The Importance of Forgiveness

"... and let them pardon and overlook. Would you not like that Allah should forgive you? And Allah is Forgiving and Merciful." **[Quran 24:22]**

The willingness to forgive is a sign of spiritual and emotional maturity. It is one of the great virtues to which we all should aspire. Imagine a world filled with individuals willing both to apologize and to accept an apology. The power of forgiveness in marriage cannot be understated. Once married, it is inevitable that you will rub each other up the wrong way as we are imperfect people.

The truth is, unless you let go, unless you forgive yourself, unless you forgive the situation, unless you realise that the situation is over, you cannot move forward to the next level. If a relationship or a marriage is built on a foundation that has no room to forgive, there won't be much to build on from there. With every mistake there will be an argument, and with every argument, the issue will go unresolved. Time and again, the past issues will re-surface again when you least expect it.

Forgiveness must be immediate, whether or not a person asks for it. Trust must be built over time and it requires a track record. It shouldn't be an occasional act but a consistent attitude, and that is when it bears the most fruit. When a person exercises forgiveness, it demonstrates that they have won the battle of disciplining the Ego or the Nafs. When you win to put the Ego at its right place, you forgive with your heart and not only with your voice. It is hard work, but this is the moment when you grow spiritually and is the birth place of joy, calm, and lightness of heart.

It brings not only spiritual benefits, but physical ones too. Research has shown that stress-related backaches and stomach aches were significantly reduced among individuals who had the habit of forgiving others. The problem we have is that most of us want to forgive but do not know how to do it or even understand what it is. Forgiving is giving up the hope that the past could be any different. It is giving up this hope, not holding onto it, wishing that it could have been any other way than it actually was.

It is the practice of letting go of the past by letting go of our perception that we need to hold a grievance for the rest of our lives. If we want to hold onto grievances, we'll never really be happy, and it is mentally draining. It's a willingness to see the person in the light of love rather than in the context of what they have done, so fundamentally it means changing our perception, and letting go of the past that we thought we wanted. We can't change that past, so it means really releasing the negative perception of it and coming back to the present.

"To err is human, to forgive is divine." Everyone makes mistakes, and if we acknowledge this fact, the act of forgiveness will become easier. It is important to note that forgiveness is not some cheap trick to employ in an effort to save your marriage. It needs to be genuine, with no strings attached. When forgiveness is a constant practice your love will stay stronger and you will experience less resentment. The more willing you are to put forgiveness at the forefront of how you operate, the better off your marriage will be.

"Forgive others, not because they deserve forgiveness, but because you deserve peace." We often believe that people stay in love because of chemistry, or because they remain intrigued with each other, because of many kindnesses, or because of luck. But part of it has got to be forgiveness and gratefulness. We have to keep in mind that people often hurt others as a result of their own pain. If somebody is rude and inconsiderate, you can be almost certain that they have some unresolved issues inside.

They have some major problems, anger, resentment, or some heartache they are trying to cope with or overcome. The last thing they need is for you to make matters worse by responding angrily. We have to forgive each other; if we don't we are tying rocks to our feet, too much for our wings to carry. Forgiveness is for those who are substantial enough to move on. Once you forgive Allah's light shines upon you. The practice of forgiveness is our most important contribution to the healing of the family and community

By saying "I forgive you" you get to step outside of that resentment or anger towards your partner and open up the mental space to move past it. The longer you hold onto grudges, the crazier you will feel. Understanding that forgiveness is for your own benefit will make it easier for you to start the process. You will be able to forgive your partner unconditionally, and not use it as a power play to get something in return. For example, if they did something wrong to you before, you cannot play the "you did this to me" card whenever you want to get your way.

When you and your partner choose to forgive each other and work through your problems in an empathetic way, you are choosing love. That is what marriage is all about. This means choosing love every single day, even when it is hard. You may disagree to such an extent that you don't even want to hear them speak, but you know you love them more than allowing the argument to spiral out of control. Not only is everyone screwed up, but everyone screws up and that is why forgiveness is a key to finding happiness. Therefore forgive yourself and forgive others to find inner freedom.

9. Beautifying yourself

Whether you are a newly married couple or in your 30th year of marriage, looking attractive and appealing is essential for a happy married life. There is no prohibition on looking good; in fact, to physically beautify oneself to please one's spouse and keep them happy is not only a praiseworthy act but also a means to earn rewards from Allah. Once we embark on parenthood, we tend to forget this vital area of beautifying ourselves and end up becoming complacent. We then ask ourselves why our relationship has lost its spark.

The problem is that we may only dress well when we are doing it for others and not for our spouse. It is worthwhile to pay your spouse the same courtesy you do to others by making yourself look attractive for him or her every once in a while. Before they become parents, people in general want to be the best parent, and there is no reason why they shouldn't be. But this makes the new mother completely immersed in her children that she becomes estranged from her husband.

The mother struggles with finding a balance between her endeavours and the reality, coming face to face with the high expectations that society sets for her. Parenting is really hard, but it is the holiest duty on earth as most of the time you put their needs before your own. But making the time to look after your appearance and cleanliness is vital for the family wellbeing. There is also valid rationale for sometimes giving priority to yourself and your spouse as a couple. Stolen moments away from the little ones are crucial for your home's overall wellbeing.

It is highly beneficial to your children's' character development when you give special time to each other as a couple. The reason for this is that if our children are our only reason for being, they will grow up to be self-centred, selfish and entitled, and will not comprehend the need for giving or sharing their time or their things. We see this everywhere today in our world, we have enough of those people living amongst us already. Valuing our spouses, loving our children, and finding time for ourselves can all co-exist within a healthy marriage.

Men in particular tend to respond to visual stimulus, and they do care more about their wife's appearance all the time. If you want to live a healthy and happy married life, one in which you care for each other in the same way as the first day of your relationship, working on yourself and making yourself look attractive is the key. It also good for your children's development as experts say children can read facial expressions in their parents before they learn to speak.

Therefore, looking good assures your children, as well as increasing your self-esteem by helping you feel positive about yourself. I remember my mother telling her daughters, my sisters, that when they are feeling down, they should go and get their hair done. Some mothers feel negative about bodily changes after birth. For some women they might experience post-natal depression. The problem in fact is not that the body changes, but that your attitude towards life changes. We can learn wisdom from a tree. If you look closely at a tree, you'll notice it has knots and dead branches, just like our bodies. But overall it looks beautiful.

What we learn is that beauty and imperfection go together wonderfully. There is nothing rarer, nor more beautiful, than a woman being unapologetically herself; comfortable in her perfect imperfection. That is the true essence of beauty. The human body is the best work of art, and it is Allah's sign of creativity. Allah also loves his creations to express their beauty. It is important to take care of yourself and put an effort every day.

This shows that you do not take their attraction to you for granted. It is basic respect for the relationship. It doesn't take much; wash regularly, and dress flatteringly. Valuing our spouses, loving our children, and finding time for ourselves can all co-exist within a healthy marriage and happy family. Giving priority to the marital relationship is a key to achieving our goal of producing happy, healthy children who are independent of us. There are many married practising Muslim brothers and sisters who lose interest in taking care of themselves at home for a variety of reasons.

Firstly, once they are married to a practicing brother, sisters assume their husband won't be interested in their looks but, rather, in their imaan. They believe their beauty lies in their 'piety'. Secondly, husbands don't express their desire in seeing their wives dressed beautifully. Or, when their wives dress up, they don't bother to compliment them, which confuses the wife into thinking, "he doesn't care." The truth is beauty and piety are two separate characteristics.

Piety may add to a person's inner beauty which may be reflected in their physical appearance; however, they are independent characteristics. Allah also loves his creations to express their beauty. This was the practice of the righteous women and men of the pious predecessors, who used to devote their time to worshipping Allah and reading the Quran. Foremost among them was Aishah "Ummul Mu'miniin", although there were many others. They would wear fine clothes and jewellery at home, as well as when they were traveling, in order to make themselves look beautiful for their husbands.

Ibn Abas is an example of a sahaba who used to put great effort into looking and smelling good for his wife. It was his habit to improve his appearance for his wife and he used to say, "I dress myself up for my wife just as she makes herself pretty for me." That is a good habit to follow. It is one of the teachings of Islam that a woman should make herself look beautiful for her husband, so that her husband sees in her that which he likes.

That is one of reasons as to why it is forbidden for a woman to dress in mourning for more than three days, except in the case of her husband's death, when she is permitted to mourn for four months and ten days. We find proof of this in the hadeeth narrated by al-Bukhaari from Zainab, the daughter of Umm Salamah, who said, "I came to Zainab bint Jahsh, the wife of the Prophet (SAW) when her brother died. She called for perfume and applied it to herself, and then said:

"I am not wearing perfume because I need to, but because I heard the Messenger of Allah (SAW) saying from the minbar, "It is not permitted for a woman who believes in Allah (subhaanahu wa ta'aalaa) and the Last Day to grieve for more than three days, except for her husband, [for whom she may grieve] four months and ten days." (Fath al-Bari, 9/484)"

You should not make it a chore "everyday", but surprise him sometimes with your beautiful appearance; beautiful natural hairdo, light make-up and classy clothes.

You are not just a mother, you are a wife too, and as a wife you need to make yourself desirable. It is tough with kids, but not impossible. When you put the kids to bed, go take a shower, spend five minutes doing your hair and put on some desirable clothes. That goes for men as well. Too often men also stop trying. They stop working out, put on weight, wear t-shirts all the time just because it is comfortable, stop trimming and cleaning their nails, and neglect oral hygiene, which is especially problematic if they are smokers. To look good requires consistency.

Finally, women need to proudly wear the titles of Wife and Mother. But always remember, before you were married with children you were *yourself* and you must refuse to lose sight of yourself. You can only be good to others when you are good to yourself. Be good to yourself and others so that the days of your lifetime will feel good. Serving others for the sake of Allah without expecting anything in return gives you the feeling of fulfilment "Sa'aadah". The feeling of fulfilment is attained only when you help others, and that is what most parents do.

Always treat yourself the way you treat your client or a customer in your business with the same charm, the same seductiveness, humour and kindness. You cannot take your spouse for granted, they are not yours, and they can leave any moment through death, divorce and illness. Make an effort to water your marital tree to stay alive.

10.   <u>Dealing with In-Law issues</u>

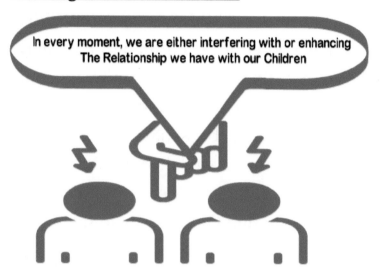

Marriage is described as a table with four legs, namely couples, children, parents and in-laws, and when any of these is broken the marriage crashes to the floor and will need to be repaired before things get out of hand. Conflict with those closest to you is always more painful than conflict with those more distant. But heathy couples deal with their in-laws by recognising they are different people with different ways.

Families have their own culture and they know culture is not bad or wrong, but different. They make an effort, even though they may not agree with or understand the family dynamics. Healthy couples also set clear boundaries with their in-laws. They're able to have open conversations with their spouse about their needs and create a plan that both of them agrees with. The challenge here will be to find the best way to say it.

For example, your partner is OK with his or her mother stopping by unannounced. You're not. So, you decide that family members need to call beforehand to make sure it's a good time to come over. Another example, for couples who live with their parents, is whether it is okay for the mother and siblings to go into their room without permission. Such conversations allow the couple to have a united front, and not battle on their own. Healthy couples separate their own relationship from their relationship with their in-laws.

This involves remembering that no matter how complicated or difficult their in-laws may be, they are not married to them. So, when the in-laws are being difficult, they make an extra effort to be kind to their spouse. They talk about their own positions and listen to each other, sympathise with each other's feelings and don't take things personally. They are able to deal with the fact that their parents are human beings, with normal and difficult human feelings, try to understand where they're coming from and empathise with them.

Apart from that, Islam has not directly given the in-laws control or claim over the wives of their sons. There are no definite rights prescribed by our religion for in-laws and the daughter-in-law is under no compulsion to obey their demands regarding her routine, her activities or her housekeeping. However, her in-laws are people who her husband loves. And the best way to settle into her husband's life is to embrace his family with love and affection.

They may have no defined rights over you; but your husband's parents do hold certain rights over you. If, for instance, you live in the same house as your in-laws, or your houses are in close proximity, your in-laws hold a very important position in your life as your neighbours. Islam has given many rights to neighbours. Even if your in-laws are not your neighbours, they are Muslims. Every Muslim has certain rights over the other, the most fundamental of which is the right of being said Salaam to giving greetings of peace. Extend the best to your in-laws and know that even if they do not respond to you, Allah will reward you.

Your mother-in-law is the one who was responsible for taking care of your husband before you came into his life. He is used to her ways, and most importantly, he's used to the food that she served him. As you master the culinary arts in your new kitchen, involve your mother-in-law and ask her to help you out. It will please her that you are taking her advice and gives her reassurance that he is in good hands. This unifies her goal and your goal and minimises the differences between you.

It will ensure that she does not feel completely isolated or replaced since your arrival into the family. It will also sow the seeds of a long and fruitful relationship with your husband's mother and your children's grandmother. Every child is close to his mother and your husband will be pleased with you for helping him love and care for his mother, who spent many difficult years raising him to be the man he is. We agree that sometimes in-laws cross boundaries when they offer advice on how to go about things and insist that their experience be taken into account.

In particular, advice on housekeeping and child-rearing leads to many ill-feelings between the mother-in-law and the daughter-in-law. The most important thing to keep in mind is to not be defensive. Listen to what they have to say, and if there is some merit or learning to be gleaned from it, do so; if it does not make sense, you are not obliged to follow what they say, but sometimes just listening to their words of advice can make them feel satisfied and you may then make your choices as you wish without any escalation.

It is also best when parents see themselves as guests in their children's marriage and fold into their rules and their lives. This leads them to be welcome, and to contribute to the emotional health of their grandchildren. For example, a wife bought her husband four non-iron shirts; his mother was with her at the time. She phoned the husband to consult him about the colours and he thanked her for her gift and her efforts. When the mother-in-law saw the label "Non-Iron Shirt", she said to her daughter-in-law, "Do you mean you don't do my son's ironing?". She replied "no, because at the moment we both work full time."

She then proceeded to tell the daughter-in-law that she still felt it was her job to do them even though both her son and daughter in-law were okay with it. These tiny issues make the relationship delicate as they are based on differing perspectives and puts them at odds with one another. As a couple, you are garments for each other as mentioned in the Quran. Garments not only adorn a person, they also protect the person and hide their blemishes and faults.

Your husband or wife's family is part of who they are. Do not talk about them to your family and friends or badmouth them. Do not share the secrets of their family with your own and do not break the trust your husband/wife has placed in you in accepting you into his/her life and opening up to you about his/her family. Every family has skeletons in the closet, and you must fulfil your role as being part of his/her family by making sure they remain safely within the closet.

Finally, the wife can play a greater role in helping her husband fulfil his responsibilities towards his parents by facilitating him, not hindering him. This does not mean that you are obliged to look after his parents for him; that is your husband's responsibility. But you can definitely help him out by extending your best behaviour and manners to them and not creating an uncomfortable atmosphere in the house. Try and give them more than what their rights are willingly, expecting your reward from Allah alone. Note that having difficulties with your in-laws doesn't mean you're in an unhealthy relationship.

11.   Avoiding Too many Debts

Home life ceases to be free and beautiful once it is founded on borrowing and debt. Debt is one of the main causes of misery in many marriages and leads to excruciating emotional pain for couples when it gets out of hand. Borrowing, and spending money you haven't got, never leads to prosperity or happiness. It is advisable to live within our means and avoid debt. Borrowing money is simply one method of deferring today's pain in exchange for repaying it with greater pain later.

Acceptance of a short period of discomfort is wiser than to mortgage a person's future. Today, there are three kinds of people: the haves, the have-nots, and the have-not-paid-for-what-they-have. The impact of debt on the relationship can actually hinder the couple's capacity to deal with the debt itself, especially if the couple can't agree on how they are going to approach it.

The entire home feels like it is on fire and it is a vicious circle. This is when husbands struggle more with their self-esteem than at any time of their lives and feel worse about themselves. The last thing they want to see is their wives nagging and turning against them. It is the difficult circumstances that push wives to do that. Wives are security-oriented and often feel afraid. Your wife really needs more affectionate hugs a day to reassure her. Open communication and a shared approach over finances are vital.

When couples adopt a united front in avoiding or solving their debt problems, the worries become minimal. You can get through hard financial times and it does not cost you your marriage. Your self-esteem will improve when you start doing something about your situation. You will be optimistic because you have a plan and can work together on it with focus and energy. This way of solving debt problems strengthens the marital relationship.

Adversity, if approached together, brings people closer, and couples express long term gratitude for one another. Men for instance always talk about how grateful they were when their wives stood by them during times of adversity. The biggest problem arises when one of the couple hides or gets into debt without their partner or family members knowing and chooses to keep the debt secret. This is mainly due to fear of blame, and of how a partner or family member will react.

The hidden debt leads to breakdown, and increases conflict, mistrust and feelings of betrayal. One of today's key developments is couples getting into debt before their marriage because they overspend on a lavish marriage ceremony. This is mainly done in order to meet societal expectations and the standards set by other families and friends. This may give short-term pleasure, but repaying the debt in the long term is psychologically taxing to the relationship.

They may even have to work overtime to repay the loan and this will have a big negative impact the quality time they intended to spend together. Worrying about repaying a loan reduces your desire for sex, which is a key to happy and healthy marital relationship. Islamic views against lavish marital ceremonies are very strong. The Prophet SAW said that the marital ceremony with the least expenditure is the most blessed. This reduces regrets and resentments later.

We have seen many lavish ceremonies which people still criticised, saying the food was salty, or the colour of the dress was not suitable for the bride, and so on. Even if you can afford such a lavish ceremony, it would have been nice to have a normal ceremony and give to poor relatives or other worthy charities. This is by far more valuable than a few likes on your Facebook and Instagram for a few days.

After a week nobody will remember such an event, the expensive dresses and sarees will remain in the wardrobe and probably have no value. If the loan or debt is an interest-based loan it is even worse as the interest accumulates. Receiving the loan statement is as painful as facing the real debtor face to face and it feels like enslavement. Interest-based loans are forbidden in all religions and constitute a greater sin. In Christianity they call this Usury; as the famous phrase of Shakespeare states, "Neither borrower nor lender be".

In Islam "Riba" is categorised as one of the seven deadliest sins. Committing such a sin by unnecessarily taking out a "Riba based loan" to pay for an extravagant wedding ceremony for example leads to misery in your marriage. There are many examples in which one or both of the couple acquired a lot of the money for their marriage ceremony via a bank loan and paying back is excruciating experience.

The husband who acquired that loan has to work so hard repaying that loan that as a result he fails to have quality time with his wife. Expectations today are very high among the younger generation in terms of care, intimacy and affection. Such emotional needs are difficult to meet when you are consumed with the worry of interest accumulating on bank loans, credit cards and overdrafts. You are not fully present in your marriage. In marital life you have to be fully present in the relationship to achieve a sense of tranquillity.

Debt can turn a free, happy person into a bitter human being, and when you are bitter the affection needed in marital life goes out of the window. It is like any other trap, easy enough to get into, but hard to get out of. When couples live so far beyond their income, they may almost be said to be living apart. Every time you borrow money, you're robbing your future self. If you can't afford it, don't get into it. If you're already in debt, get out quickly.

It is true "A poor man without a debt smiles more often than a rich man in debt". Today, debt has brought to their knees not only individuals but also countries. Historically, a man who had no debts was considered virtuous, honest, and hardworking. Today, whoever does not owe does not exist. I owe, therefore I am. Whoever is not credit-worthy deserves neither name nor face. The credit card is proof of the right to exist; debt, something even those who have nothing have. Debt means enslavement to the past.

Conclusion

It is difficult to conclude when we are writing about marriage as it is the oldest institution on Earth, starting from Adam and Eve. It demonstrates one of the signs of Allah and for that reason, it is an infinite and vast subject to write about. It will not end even if every one of us writes about it, as we are all different from one another. For example, the way you express your love might be different from others. But the principle of importance of expressing your love and respect to your spouse is well known. The aim of this book is to give you the principles that have worked for others, with some examples to elucidate them.

This allows you to act on these principles and implement them your own way. Marriage overall is a good thing. You need companions in all different areas of your life, but there is nothing like the companionship of a marriage.

You need to be willing to pay the price to make your marriage successful and tranquil. It requires selflessness, devotion and commitment. Before marriage, our most pressing daily concern is the satisfaction of our own needs and desires. We only discover our worst characteristics, impatience and immaturity, when we get married.

That is why marriage is a transformation; you become something other than you were before. Your very identity changes, as you are bonded for life to this other person. You will discover how little you had learned in your single life and how little you had grown. Only when you become a parent and a spouse do you learn to see yourself, and only that time will you learn to forget yourself. That is the true beauty of this institution. You discover what it means to really take joy in someone else; in their happiness, in their accomplishments and in their victories.

It is vital we understand the fundamentals of this great institution of marriage. Understanding it allows you to figure out that real love in marriage is not, as people claim, experienced as "love at first sight". You will acknowledge you were infatuated with her at first sight. Every marriage starts this way, but it cannot survive in the long run. The love that will take you a long way is defined by commitment, sacrifice, and devotion, and none of those dimensions is present when you first meet. You do not fall into it, but you promise it, make it, build it and fight for it.

Love is dying to the self or it represents the death of Ego self, it is the accumulation of small things that happen in the relationship and none of them happen by accident. It is those little things like getting them a juice or cappuccino when you were making yours without them asking. Another example could be speaking well of them in front of family or friends.

There will always be a dry seasons in your marital life. During this period, you may feel little attraction and affection. But successful couples still have their love intact. They love because they understand that love is an act of devotion, and they are not relieved from the duty of that devotion just because they no longer feel all warm inside.

This takes a lot of courage and is the only way to make the journey into the great beyond, to "marital tranquillity". This is where you feel with your spouse the same way, or close to, how a parent loves their children. We may sometimes not feel affectionate towards our kids, but we still love them. There will be no conditions attached to the love we have publicly pledged. We start to love unconditionally, and nobody is more entitled to it than your spouse, as you are in debt to her/him.

The most important thing for couples to master is understanding the behavioural differences between male and female and how these differences can complement each other without any conflict. We need to recognise the differences in the way God designed men and women. They are differences that He intended for good but sometimes we do not realise they exist, or do not see them as legitimate. Men and women are equal in the sight of god, but that does not mean we are the same. One key to a fulfilling marriage is to work with His design rather than against it.

Both men and women have their differing insecurities. For women, they need reassurance of being worthy of loving, that they are loveable and special. A woman wants her husband to tell her in words and in action that she is important, special and unique to you. She needs affection more than sex. In fact affection is what leads to her desire to have sex with you.

One of our problems as a man is, we just want to go for the goal without affection. It does no feel right for women that way, and that is why many men say that they feel as if they are raping their wives. The reason is that they are eating unripe fruits; it is affection that makes her ripe for sex and affection is not expensive at all.

Affection is not buying expensive stuff, but those small accumulating acts and words that you express to demonstrate that this relationship means a lot to you. It can be dropping everything you are doing just to make certain she is all right. Plenty of hugs and kisses, a steady flow of words, common courtesies and meaningful gifts to show you are thinking of her and value her presence in your life. The best way to show affection is when you give your full attention when she is expressing herself, as she has much within her she wants to share. You should talk to her at the level of feeling and not just the level of knowledge and info.

She needs you to listen to her thoughts and feelings about the events of her day with sensitivity and concern whilst resisting the temptation to offer solutions. It is important for the husband to recognise the wife's God-given strengths. Otherwise he will be weak in those areas, as she is designed to supply what he lacks.

Similarly, it is vital for the wife to understand that the primary needs of males, including husbands are respect, recreational companionship and sex. The need for respect is at the core of his self-esteem, and it affects every other area of his life. A wife can demonstrate this by understanding his value and achievement and reminding him his capabilities. This shows that the wife is proud of her husband, not out of duty, but as an expression of sincere admiration. This is what makes husband get out of his comfort zone and achieve great things in life. Most of the great achievers in history always acknowledge those sacrifices and contributions.

In life we always look for ourselves not knowing we are who we have been looking for; I mean self-knowledge. This is where our spouses help us, and the message they convey to us is treat yourself like someone you love, be gentle on yourself and face your fears. In this way you will learn that the only obstacle to yourself is you "inner critic" and you are the only one who can make you happy.

I remember how a simple text from my wife reversed my fear of public speaking. I always dreaded doing presentations, and thought of myself as a piece of meat, and the audience as lions that wanted to eat me. As I was entering the train station to the University to do my presentation, I received a text in the Somali language from my wife: "Go for it and share your wisdom, I Love you". That enabled me to overcome my fears of speaking in front of a huge lecture theatre audience. I delivered an impactful presentation that night and there was fruitful discussions

All my thoughts were focused on sharing my ideas with the audience and at no single moment did I think of myself. It is at best when you are in a giving mode as that is the best route to feeling fulfilled "give in order to get". I still have a fear of public speaking but am more comfortable with accommodating and accepting it.

Today, people even have a fear of getting married; the younger generation are hesitant to get married and start families because they think they are not cut out for it. The younger generation are delaying longer than any generation before. There is no doubt that they are now the most marriage-averse in human history. This is a dangerous legacy, because it represents a rejection of an institution that is integral to our advancement as a species. Therefore, I urge you to face your fears as the plane faces the wind to fly. My advice to you is to disregard the toxic flaw in the philosophy of *"I will get married once everything is perfect in my life"*.

As human being, we are works in progress even though we think we are finished product. We are not finished product yet and in need to build the bridge on we must cross the river of life. To achieve that, the intention must come from you "Within" and it is tough journey. But getting married is one of those challenges you get into that facilitates to build a solid bridge. Difficulty is essential in life and embracing it is vital for a fulfilling life. Allah has mentioned clearly in the Quran the human beings will be tested, as life is full of trials and tribulation.

Those who navigate through such challenges with patience and perseverance will be victorious. Life is never perfect, and never will be. Marriage gives you the wonderful opportunity to traverse the ups and downs with your husband or wife beside you. To wait until everything is perfect in your life has its own consequences and is one of the causes of the high rate of preventable divorce cases.

Challenges never go for good, and when they reappear some couples look for the nearest exit, stating *"I did not sign up for this"*. There is a beauty in imperfection and accepting and accommodating to it is a great wisdom. Psychologists argue that one of the causes of reluctance to take on challenges for many is rooted in a time in childhood, when you were praised for your ability and were bombarded with statements like "Wow, you got (X many) right. That is really good score. You must be smart at this.

They argue that such statements create a fixed mind-set in children. *In their research, when they gave (those praised for their ability) a new challenging task, the children rejected participating.* They did not want to do anything that could expose their flaws and call into question their talent. *In contrast, those students who were praised for effort, 90 percent of them wanted the challenging new task that they could learn from and developed a growth mindset.*

Just as there are no great achievement without setbacks, there are no great relationships without conflict and problems along the way. We need to cultivate a growth mind-set so that we can acknowledge our partner's imperfections, without assigning blame and still feel we have a fulfilling relationship. We need to see conflicts as problems of communication, not of personality or character.

In Japan when a piece of pottery is broken, they do not throw it away. They repair it by mending the areas of breakage with lacquer dusted or mixed with powdered gold, silver or platinum. This gives the pottery a new lease of life and even makes it more beautiful than it was before. Similarly, every time you mend your marriage wholeheartedly, it takes both of you to another level, better than before. That is why some parents give their children a beautiful repaired pot when they reach adulthood. This will be a gift of optimism to them.

Life is our own tale of adventures and triumphs. I hope when you encounter the real trials of life, like mended pots you will not be afraid to show your scars; that is the beauty of imperfection. This enables you to be totally up for challenges and face them constructively. This will lead you move from the dark hour at night to the morning sunshine. That is the time you will say, it was worth facing marriage at younger age.

Youth is a gift as it comes with health, energy and vitality. These attributes give you purpose and promise in your younger years. The problem today is that these qualities are wasted and channelled to the wrong place. We are using our energy to become more passionate consumers and devoting them to our employer in the name of being more perfect servants to our corporate masters. Having said this, many young people woke up during the financial crisis of 2008 and acknowledged that this is not worthy adventure.

After the financial crisis there has been growing number of youths getting married and having children. Because of this growing trend, many corporate organisations like Facebook and Apple announced the offer of a 'health benefit' up to $20,000 for egg freezing for female employees and a host of other fertility services for male and female employees. To me it is a terrible thing to treat marriage and children as burdens which can be left to come back to at a convenient time.

The actual social skills and emotional intelligence that are in demand in today's market can be acquired from raising family. It is inherent in us always to long for and wish to love, to fight and live for something. We urge you to marry and try to detoxify yourself from romantic capitalism and unrealistic expectations. This has born out of the huge change in our social structure and fabrics. There is no longer communal living and these changes have impacted our traditional bearing.

These changes can be summarised in three processes. Firstly, a process of rationalization of scientific research, which has accelerated technical progress. Secondly, a process of political democratization, which has fostered individual rights. And thirdly, a process of rationalization of economic production and of trade liberalisation.

These three intertwined processes have created radical consequences for the individual. Now individuals are free to value or disvalue any attitude, any choice, any object· Today we are asking or expecting from our partner what an entire village used to provide, these include "Give me belonging, identity, continuity, transcendence, mystery and awe, comfort, edge, novelty, familiarity, predictability and give me surprise all in one". The desire of being desired becomes the ultimate goal and to remain desirable and sustain it is the most difficult part. This is due to our inability to reconcile love and desire. *Love means to "Have" whereas desire means to "Want". In love, we want to have, we want to know the beloved, minimize the distance and we want closeness.*

But in desire, we tend to not really want to go back to the places we've already gone. Forgone conclusion does not keep our interest. The only way to sustain desire is to give space as desire needs space. That is why you desire your spouse more when you travel abroad and watching them from a distance when they perform. Our need for togetherness exists alongside our need for separateness. One does not exist without the other. In spiritual term, it is dangerous to follow your desires only, as it is not sustainable. Following our desires without self-control is our greatest limitation as a human being and this is the shift in culture we are experiencing today. We have shifted from a culture of humility to the culture what you might call "Big Me" or "Ego driven".

We moved away from a culture that encouraged to think humbly of themselves to a culture that encouraged people to see themselves as the centre of the universe. We hear clichés such as *"follow your passion", "don't accept limits" and "chart your own course"*. Such clichés require a touch of humility.

The problem with this is, it creates an obstacle of overeager desire to have people think about you. It leads to so many things such as:

- Selfishness: Desire to use other people as means to get things for yourself.
- Pride: Desire to see our self as superior to everybody else.
- Ignore and rationalise our own imperfections and inflate your virtues.
- Constantly seeking recognition, and painfully sensitive to any snub or insult to the status we believe we have earned for ourselves. All of the above traits make us so fragile within and negatively impacts our marriage.

Therefore, we need to exercise humility in every aspect of our lives. Humility is a soil in which pride does not easily grow. It is freedom from the need to prove you are superior all the time. This is real liberation and your creativity level will go up.

It is the awareness that there is a lot of what you think you know is distorted or wrong. This allows to put yourself in the "Centre stage" of your thoughts to gain prospective on your own ways of feeling, thinking and acting. In the course of this confrontation with ourselves we build character and achieve inner cohesion. This will finally lead us not to crumble in adversity and our minds are consistent and dependable.

I hope you benefited from this book. My goal before I die was to leave this short book behind and at least succeed in saving and improving one couple's marriage. It is said when you are ready to learn, the teacher will appear. I ask Allah to make this book one of those teachers who will appear for couples to learn this great and magnificent institution "Marriage "and join its journey with joy. May Allah accept it from all of us "Amin.

The end.

If you are interested in watching animation videos covering marital relationship subjects. Please feel free to visit my Facebook page below:

https://www.facebook.com/developyournation/